**World Council
of Churches**

VOLOS ACADEMY
FOR THEOLOGICAL
S T U D I E S

HOLY METROPOLIS OF DEMETRIAS

MANY WOMEN WERE ALSO THERE...

Cover design: Indiktos Publications, Greece
FRIDA KAHLO, «The Flower Basket», 1941 (Detail)

WCC ISBN 978-2-8254-1559-7

© 2010 WCC Publications, World Council of Churches
150 route de Ferney, P.O. Box 2100
1211 Geneva 2, Switzerland
Website: www.oikoumene.org

Volos Academy For Theological Studies
P.O. Box 1308, 380 01 Volos, Greece
Website: www.acadimia.gr

ISBN 978-960-518-384-4

Printed in Greece

MANY WOMEN WERE ALSO THERE...

THE PARTICIPATION OF ORTHODOX WOMEN
IN THE ECUMENICAL MOVEMENT

Editors:
ELENI KASSELOURI-HATZIVASSILIADI
FULATA MBANO MOYO
AIKATERINI PEKRIDOU

WORLD COUNCIL OF CHURCHES PUBLICATIONS
Geneva, Switzerland

VOLOS ACADEMY FOR THEOLOGICAL STUDIES
Volos, Greece

"The female face of Orthodox Christianity is largely unknown and is still to be explored"

ELISABETH BEHR-SIGEL

CONTENTS

FOREWORD
Pantelis Kalaitzidis[1]

It is a privilege for me to write a foreword to *"'Many women were also there...' The Participation of Orthodox Women in the Ecumenical Movement"*. This collection of 18 essays represents the work of Orthodox women from various historical and social contexts, with a plurality of concerns and priorities. It comes at a crucial moment for Orthodoxy, a moment when the last is called to enter into a sincere dialogue with the multicultural and multifaith societies and intellectuals, especially on issues like the role of the laity and women in the life of the Church.

We cannot deny the fact that many Orthodox churches are experiencing a serious problem – or a great ecclesiological paradox: that is, the lack of laity participation and the dominance of the clergy in the Church. This reality finds its natural sequel in the prevalent viewpoint within ecclesiastical and theological circles on the role of women in the Church. However, it would not be far from the truth to say that the downgraded position of women in current Orthodox ecclesiastical circumstances is part of the broad problem known as "the (non) participation of laity in Church life". It is not without reason that many acknowledge the increasing alienation of the ecclesial body from theology as well as the inability to establish dialogue between theology, academia, and the modern world.

We must note that the new and radical element that characterized theology and the praxis of the Christian Church from the very beginning– as a result of its Eucharistic and eschatological identity –was the overcoming of all kinds of division and fragmentation (gender, tribe, nation, language, culture, social class and origin), to the extent that

---

1. Dr Pantelis Kalaitzidis is a well-known Orthodox scholar and the Director of the Volos Academy for Theological Studies of the Holy Metropolis of Demetrias.

"there is no longer Jew or Greek, there is no longer slave or free, there is no longer male and female; for all of you are one in Christ Jesus" (Gal., 3:28. Cf. Col., 3:11). Therefore, it was only natural that the early church re-valued the place of women, as is explicitly demonstrated in several biblical texts as well as in the praxis of the early Christian community. Also, later patristic tradition in the person of St Gregory of Nazianzus was to repeat and expand Paul's theology of unity and its eschatological fulfillment in Christ. In this, there is no place for any segmentation or division whatsoever, to such an extent that Gregory characterizes gender, tribe or social class discrimination as "traits of flesh" that demean the Christ-likeness and image of God in human beings.

Christianity, in contrast to the ideas and practices of the male-dominated Hebraic and Ancient-Greek milieu in which it appeared, re-valued the role of woman. In the person of a woman, the Theo-tokos Mary, a human being was counted worthy, within history, to give birth to the Son and Word of God. Eminent representatives of Christian Tradition, such as St Gregory Nazianzus, did not hesitate to denounce the unjust laws towards women: "laws were enacted by men; therefore, legislation would be against women; ... I don't embrace this legislation, nor do I praise this practice". The texts and speeches of St John Chrysostom express for the first time a theology of tenderness in marriage and, concerning the attitude of husband towards wife, he stressed the communion of persons, and the priority of companion-ship, mutual attraction and love rather than childbearing being the prime aim of marriage.

In addition, the missionary activity, the liturgical and social func-tion, and the life of the first Christian communities in general perhaps for the very first time in history led to women moving outside the home. They took on roles or vocations within the Christian church parallel to those of traditional wife and mother: for example, as mis-sionary, as charismatic or as social worker. Moreover, the establish-ment of the institution of deaconess in the early church and throughout almost the entire Byzantine period witnesses this new reality, and invites the Church, if she wishes to remain true to her tradition, to think hard about and begin a dialogue on the revival of this ancient apostolic order.

However, this new dimension of reality did not outlast the burden of Hebraic mores and traditions, social conservatism, and established philosophical and anthropological prejudice, mainly of ancient Greek origin, that influenced the church's historical course and praxis. Indeed, parallel to the liberating attitude we presented in brief, the tendency to belittle and disdain women –to associate them with evil, sin and smut– was not missing from church circles. References to women's silence in church and their subordination to men are repeated by St Basil of Caesarea, commenting on the respective quotation of Paul, and in a milder tone by Gregory of Nazianzus, in a text attributed to him in *Sacra Parallela* by John of Damascus. Even St John Chrysostom, who, inaugurating a theology of tenderness, speaks so warmly about relations within marriage and the love of husbands for wives – elsewhere has difficulty applying to woman the basic anthropological principle of "in God's image".

It is also widely known that negative expressions and characterizations of women are abundant in ascetic texts, to the extent that women are considered more dangerous and vicious than the devil himself. In church pre-christening services relating to birth and the forty days following birth, there are reference to smuttiness and uncleanness that presuppose the biological function of maternity as "impure": in these, sexual intercourse is demonized and women degraded and humiliated. These were the perceptions that led to the establishment of the well-known interdictions and legal provisions that regard the female body and female menstruation in a totally negative way, rendering woman a second-category member of the church and introducing the shadow and the burden of the Law within the church.

Moreover, the hierarchical subordination of women to men –the "heritage" of the ancient-Greek and Judaic world –passed to a certain extent through the institutions, life and spirituality of the Church, especially monastic spirituality, reproducing forms and structures that were evidently not in correspondence with its theological and eschatological self-consciousness, leading from time to time to the temptation of fundamentalism. The depressing burden of history and social conformism was often more of a weight in the history of the Church than evangelical truth and authenticity, as witnessed by the current ecclesiastical and pastoral reality, which is far from friendly towards women.

Can the Church and theology, therefore, continue to refer gloatingly to the first reality and pretend that they don't care about the second? Can we close off all current related discussions about the role of women in the church while claiming continually and unilaterally that Christianity has liberated women when after twenty centuries so many questions are still pending? Further, even the limited dignity and equality enjoyed by women nowadays seem to be more a result and consequence of the conquests of the Enlightenment and "modernity" (which would be unconceivable, in our opinion, if it were not for its Christian origins) and of the women's movement after the 19th century than a result and consequence of the traditional "Christian" communities.

The crucial question that follows is how long we will continue to accept, as self-evident and in howling contradiction with our ecclesiological and theological self-consciousness, and justify theologically the social construction of gender, the male-dominated/patriarchic relations of power, and the domination resulting from this structure despite the fact that civil society and secular institutions consider all of this obsolete? Would not a theological consideration of gender and of "in the image of God" in women, in combination with the theological and pastoral exploitation that overcomes the distinction of pure-impure, inaugurated by the New Testament manage to interpret the tough theological and social problems posed by the issue under discussion?

As the book's focus is on the participation of Orthodox women in the ecumenical movement, let us remember that Orthodox theology in the 20th century has developed and become known, as well as rediscovering its self-consciousness and its mission in the world in the framework of ecumenical dialogue, through its encounter with the questions, concerns and challenges posed by the West. We have to recognize the significant contribution of the ecumenical movement, and especially of the World Council of Churches (WCC), as far as women's issues are concerned. The previous meetings of Orthodox women in Damascus and Istanbul and the publication of the book, as the fruit of those meetings, *Orthodox Women Speak: Discerning the "Signs of the Times"* are of great importance.

More than a decade after that publication, the present volume provides Orthodox and other Christians with many new perspectives on the role of Orthodox women in the church, theology and ecumenical movement. We hope that the voices of the 45 women who came together in Volos Consultation two years ago and those who contributed to the volume will be heard by their churches in order that they, as Paul writes, "not be conformed to this world, but be transformed by the renewing of our minds, so that we may discern what is the will of God – what is good and acceptable and perfect" (Rom. 12:2).

PREFACE
FULATA MBANO MOYO

I write this preface humbly acknowledging that this book provides space for Orthodox women to reflect on what participation in the ecumenical movement entails for them with the particularity of their Orthodox Tradition that roots back to the beginnings of the Church. How do I, an African woman of Reformed Tradition justify my sharing of this space? One simple answer would be that the Orthodox women honoured me with their acceptance of me as their sister in the ecumenical journey towards visible unity-an expression of deep Christian hospitality. As different but equal in the sight of God, this acceptance also challenges me to offer similar hospitality to others. Leaning on my reformed sister's wisdom, Letty Mandiville Russell's language of just hospitality, I can also say the follows:

> Being a misfit allows us to understand the meaning of hospitality and honor difference from the side of the stranger... As an advocate of peace with justice, I can work with others for empowerment of all peoples, "regardless." (2009: 13).

Since 2007 when I joined WCC taking up the responsibility of "Women in Church and Society", working with Orthodox women has offered me a safe but enduring challenge of the reality of diversity in the way women participate in the different ministries of the Church. As someone who has been shaped by a particular reformed understanding of women being part of "a priesthood of every believer," which sometimes seem to narrow this understanding to women's ordination, the different but equally enriching ways in which Orthodox women have understood their participation in the Church and the ecumenical movement has helped me to widen my own understanding of being different but one. Planning and anticipating the Volos Academy meeting that has given rise to this publication brought that challenge home as I experienced the acceptance with which I worked together with my Orthodox sister, Dr Eleni Kasselouri-Hatzivassiliadi in shaping this meeting. Volos gathering brought the richness of diversity even within the Orthodox tradition as women with commitment to and love for their church reflected on issues of concern so as to meaningfully contribute to the continued journey towards unity. The venue of Volos Academy was God's perfect gift for such reflections. The committed presence of Dr Pantelis Kalaitzidis throughout this gathering gave me extra hope knowing that the concern of Orthodox women participation in the ecumenical movement was shared with Orthodox men as well because it was about being church together as a community of women and men. The blessings through the greeting and address by H.E. Metropolitan of Demetrias & Almyros Ignatios gave an assurance that these reflections were done by the complete blessings of the church. All these were important introduction to my work with the Orthodox women, which remains at the core of WCC "Women in Church and Society" initiatives for the participation of women in the ecumenical movement.

From the history of Orthodox women participation in the ecumenical movement to addressing some issues of concern as violence against women within the Decade to Overcome Violence and Orthodox women's participation in the 21st century, the reflections women share in this book offer deep insights to questions of the ecumenical process of building just and peaceable communities of women and men, young and old as the churches' response to Jesus' call "that we may all be one!" (John 17:11). Within the context of the Decade to Overcome Violence, through these pages, Orthodox women have meaningfully shared their Christian spirituality of resilience, healing and wholeness exploring the historical contributions of Orthodox women and saints include the most recent contributions of Elisabeth Behr-Sigel, whose decade since her death we hope to commemorate with a gathering of Orthodox women and men in conversation with men and women of other Christian traditions in 2011 in Strasbourg,

France. Towards the May 2011 International Ecumenical Peace Convocation and the 10th Assembly in 2013, Orthodox women's participation brings rich perspectives to the ecumenical debate especially as we wrestle with what unity and just peace entails in our world today.

INTRODUCTION

ELENI KASSELOURI-HATZIVASSILIADI

" *Many women were also there…" The Participation of Orthodox Women in the Ecumenical Movement* is the collection of the papers offered during the consultation held in Volos, Greece, 8-12 June 2008, which was organized by the World Council of Churches (WCC) programme on "Women in Church and Society" and hosted by the Volos Academy for Theological Studies and the Holy Metropolis of Demetrias. To these papers some new essays were added, written by the new generation of Orthodox women theologians who attended the consultation but, due to limitations of time, did not present a lecture.

The idea and the proposal of organizing a consultation on the topic of Orthodox women's participation in the ecumenical movement came from previous meetings of the WCC program on Women's Voices and Visions on Being Church. Aruna Gnanadason, who led the programme, organized various meetings in different regions around the world. The Orthodox women who participated brought up again and again the question of organizing a meeting to evaluate their participation in the ecumenical movement and simultaneously to plan future activities, initiatives and ways of strengthening this involvement. The need for an inter-Orthodox women's network was at the heart of the discussions. In the last inter-Orthodox meeting of women before Volos, which took place 11-16 October 2001 in Geneva, thirteen Orthodox women from Albania, Australia, Bulgaria, Cyprus, France, Greece, Lebanon, Romania, the USA, and the WCC discussed their understanding of the Church; encouraged Orthodox women theologians, historians, sociologists, psychologists and health care providers to publish their writings and editors of scholarly journals to be more receptive to their research; and, finally, noted that they would like to see "Orthodox women organize themselves on an international level into a formal network" that would have a close relationship with and be supported by the bishops and the priests of the church.

The consultation in Volos came seven years after the meeting in Geneva and more than ten years after the meetings in Damascus and Istanbul. The Holy Metropolis of Demetrias, H.E. Metropolitan Ignatios, and the Volos Academy for Theological Studies, where I have had the pleasure and the privilege of working since 2007, considered it an honor to host such an important consultation. Especially for the Volos Academy for Theological Studies and its academic team, the participation of women in the life of the Church and the issue of the participation of the laity are two of the most crucial and "burning" themes the Orthodox churches have to deal with in the 21st century. The Academy, for that reason, had already dedicated two academic years to discussing them: "Gender and Religion: The Role of Women in the Church" in 2002-03 and "The Participation of the Laity in the Life of the Church" in 2003-04.

In the Volos consultation, the WCC general secretariat and the programme on "Women in Church and Society" officially invited delegates from Eastern and Oriental Orthodox churches. They also invited well-known Orthodox women theologians, who participated in the various programmes of WCC and wrote about Orthodox women's participation in the ecumenical movement and in the Orthodox Church. Finally, Orthodox women who work in ecumenical bodies or represent their churches in committees of WCC and CEC were also invited. The number went up to 45 women: from Europe, the USA, Australia, Asia and the Middle East.

Many speakers stressed that issues on women's participation in the Church and society are very often discussed in the framework of ecumenical gatherings, especially those of the WCC. From the very beginning, WCC was encouraged by the YWCA and other women's ecumenical bodies to give systematic attention to evaluating the worldwide ministry of women. As W.A. Vissert Hooft commented, "unless women are given more responsibility in the life of their local churches, the renewal cannot be achieved"[1]. These words, according to Pauline Webb, proved prophetic. In the second half of the 20th century, the concern and the questions about the participation of women in the life of the Church became a focus of ecumenical controversy. Parallel to this debate has been the growing awareness of the special gifts of women, of feminist insights in theology, and of the mutual enrichment that comes through full partnership in ministry and service in both family and community. The Ecumenical Decade: Churches in Solidarity with Women (1988-98 EDCSW) was an opportunity for the churches and the ecumenical movement to transform into action the many commitments they had made to women since the WCC came into being. In the frame of the EDCSW, two main inter-Orthodox gatherings took place: one in Damascus (1995) and the second in Istanbul (1997). Aruna Gnanadason describes her experience from these gatherings in her preface in the book *Orthodox Women Speak: Discerning the "Signs of the Times"*:

> I learned from my Orthodox sisters what it means to for us as women to love the Church and to respect its great traditions and yet speak with courage and conviction when something there disturbs us. All the women I met at these meetings are indeed gifts to the ecumenical movement. The Orthodox women spoke with sensitivity and respect and yet with boldness. It taught me that women can speak from within Tradition, yet also speak to the Tradition and be part of the transformation of Tradition[2].

1. Pauline Webb, "Women in Church and Society", in *Dictionary of the Ecumenical Movement*, WCC Publications, Geneva, 2002, p. 1208-11, esp. 1209.
2. Preface, in Kyriaki Karidoyannes FitzGerald (ed.), *Orthodox Women Speak. Discerning the "Signs of the Times"*, WCC Publications/Holy Cross Orthodox Press, 1999, p. x.

The Volos consultation brought together –and this was one of the intentions of the organizers– three generations of Orthodox women. First was the generation that worked in the EDCSW, and participated in the inter-Orthodox Rhodos consultation (1988), the Crete meeting, Damascus and the Istanbul conferences. Then there was the generation that continued with the WCC programme on Women Voices and Visions. And last, but not least, was the third generation of young women theologians who are active today in various ecumenical bodies, giving witness for their tradition and faith. Bringing the three generations together in dialogue was neither an easy nor an impassive enterprise. This common journey was not without difficulties and challenges. The authoritative language used by some representatives of the older generation often became an obstacle for the spontaneous, free and full participation of the younger. However, the whole process was an interesting learning experience for all and an opportunity to realize that in order to move forward we need an ethos of humility, sincerity, mutual trust, love and forgiveness. A true and honest dialogue should always invite everyone as equals into a process of learning to listen rather than to simply speak.

During the conference, all the so-called open issues were discussed; those, in other words, that require a deeper theological analysis and comprehension by the Orthodox. Among them were: the revival of female diaconate, the more active participation of women in the administrative and pastoral work of the church, the empowerment of women in theological research and study, and the language and content of some liturgical texts connected with women. The contribution of WCC in the continuation of the theological discussion is vital. As a platform for dialogue, WCC, according to the Orthodox women, should continue to support the inter-Orthodox and inter-Christian dialogue among women; provide resources for research and study; and offer its help and knowledge in the creation of an inter-Orthodox women's network. Additionally, it is important for Orthodox women to receive the full support of the Orthodox church leadership. These leaders should together identify the ways and instruments to put decisions and recommendations of women into practice and in this way change attitudes and habits that discriminate and subordinate women.

The publication of these papers in a volume was a request and a demand that came from the participants. The last Orthodox women's publication that derived from meetings was the already-mentioned *Orthodox Women Speak: Discerning the "Signs of the Times"*, edited by Kyriaki Karidoyanes FitzGerald (WCC Publications/Holy Cross, 1997). The book *Women's Voices and Visions of the Church: Reflections of Orthodox Women*, edited by Sophie Deicha, Cristina Breaban and Eleni Kasselouri-Hatzivassiliadi (WCC, 2006) was a publication of that particular WCC programme and in no way connected with an inter-Orthodox consultation or gathering.

The present volume is composed of three parts and thematic groupings of papers. The first part accommodates the historical and theological essays on the participation of Orthodox women in the ecumenical movement and the life of the Orthodox church. The second part contains essays on how women can be examples of theological and spiritual excellency and sources of inspiration and encouragement for the rest. The third part hosts the voices coming from particular contexts and local needs, challenges, initiatives, and actions. Although different in content and structure, all the essays constitute a critical, deep, penetrating and honest look at Orthodox women's participation in ecumenism and the life of local communities.

Both, the consultation and the book would have been impossible without the generosity and the collaboration of love, common trust and mutual tolerance of many people. I would like first of all to express my deep feelings of appreciation to Dr Fulata Mbano Moyo for her trust, her faith to our common vision for unity, and mainly for her wisdom and strength to always forgive human weakness. I thank H.E. Bishop Ignatios for his spiritual guidance and his willingness to support ecumenical efforts for the unity of all; the director of the Volos

Academy, Dr Pantelis Kalaitzidis, my colleague and brother in Christ for his vision for theology and the Church; my colleagues in 2008: Katerina Karkala-Zorba, Anastasia Vassiliadi, Aikaterini Pekridou, Claire Nikolaou, Niko Ntonto, Arseni Arsenaki, and Christo Parisi; and my colleagues in 2010: Valila Giannoutaki and Nikolao Asprouli. I would also like deeply to thank the WCC publications office and especially Mr Michael West, Mr Mark Beach, and Mrs Colette Stoeber; also Mrs Maria Cristina Rendon for her patience and kindness in answering all my "strange" administrative questions; the Indiktos Publications, and especially its director Manolis Velitzanidis, for designing the beautiful cover and printing the book. And finally my deepest appreciation to all the contributors of the volume for their hard work, inspiration, dedication to the vision of a Church as "a community of faith, hope and love, of men and women, of mysterious human persons, unutterably equal yet different, made in the image and reflecting the glory of God, the Three in One"[3].

3. Elisabeth Behr-Sigel & Kallistos Ware, *The Ordination of the Women in the Orthodox Church*, WCC Publications, Geneva, 2000, p.10.

ADDRESS TO THE CONSULTATION
H.E. METROPOLITAN OF DEMETRIAS & ALMYROS IGNATIOS

Beloved Sisters in Christ,
We welcome you warmly to the Holy Metropolis of Demetrias & Almyros and the city of Volos. It is a great pleasure for us to host a consultation of 45 Orthodox women, who are official delegates of other Eastern and Oriental Orthodox churches and well-known theologians, on the topic *"'Many women were also there...' The Participation of Orthodox Women in the Ecumenical Movement: Past, Present, Future".*

We should express our deep appreciation to the Women's Programme of the World Council of Churches (WCC) and especially to Dr Fulata Mbano Moyo for providing the necessary support for the organization of this consultation. I would like also to offer my personal thanks to the Director of the Volos Academy for Theological Studies, Dr Pantelis Kalaitzidis, the members of its academic team, and especially to Dr Eleni Kasselouri-Hatzivassiliadi for the initiation. The Volos Academy, a local institution of our Metropolis, has been from the very beginning sensitive to and much interested in issues on the participation of women in the life of the Church. The Academy dedicated the entire academic year of 2002-2003 to examining and discussing the role of women in the Church, and the theological challenges, concerns and ambivalences of this topic.

The New Testament verse "Many women were also there..." (Mat. 27:55) reminds us of the important role that women played in the history of the Church and in the installation and spread of the gospel. Mary, who is the first among all (Mat. 1;18) – the Mother of our Lord, Theotokos, the "more honorable than the Cherubim" according to our liturgical tradition – answers positively to God's invitation and becomes "the bridge that carries people from earth to heaven". The catalogue of women in our church is endless: women apostles who transfer the message of Jesus' resurrection, the saints, the martyrs, the nuns, the teachers in faith, the Holy Mothers. Modern women, as active members of our churches, continue to offer a witness (*martyria*) of the Orthodox Tradition to our multicultural and multifaith societies in various ways.

We have to confess that the Orthodox church did not avoid the temptation –and this is common in other Christian denominations as well– to "exploit" women in practice in various ways. The twenty-fifth of the conclusions of the inter-Orthodox symposium in Rhodos (1988) points out and admits this fact,

> While recognizing these facts, which witness to the promotion through the Church of the equality of honour between men and women, it is necessary to confess in honesty and with humility, that, owing to human weakness and sinfulness, the Christian communities have not always and in all places been able to suppress effectively ideas, manners, customs, historical developments and social conditions *which have resulted in practical discrimination against women*[1].

Although Jesus praised Mary for sitting and listening to the word (Lk. 10:38-42), the church more often has given a priority to and preferred Martha's role for women in its life. However, our historical and social contexts and era demand from the woman, the wife, the mother and the professional a combination of Martha's and Mary's roles: that is, to "worry and be distracted by many things" but also to "choose the better part" (Lk. 10:41-42). Our Orthodox churches should not remain silent and voiceless in front of the modern challenges; rather, after discerning the "signs of the times", they should support and empower the many-faced role of Orthodox women in the Church and society.

---

1. See Genadios Limouris (ed.), *The Place of the Woman in the Orthodox Church and the Question of the Ordination of Women*, Tertios Publications, 1992, p. 29.

Your consultation is going to examine and evaluate another important sphere in which Orthodox women have been called to be active in the 20th and 21th centuries: that of the ecumenical dialogue. All Orthodox churches that participate in the ecumenical movement have realized the necessity of women's presence in their delegations and the important role of women in theological, administrative, social and pastoral work of the Church. I am convinced that with small, perhaps at times hesitant, steps we continue walking toward the realization and experience of the vision that is so beautifully expressed by Leontios, Bishop of Neapolis of Cyprus: "If we are all equal in Christ, we should become equal to each other".

I am looking forward to hearing your concerns, proposals and conclusions. May our Lord Jesus Christ and his Holy Mother Virgin Mary always strengthen your special gifts, wisdom and willingness for the transformation of church life and the whole world.

REPORT OF THE INTER-ORTHODOX CONSULTATION "AND MANY WOMEN WERE ALSO THERE..." (MATH. 27:55) PARTICIPATION OF ORTHODOX WOMEN IN THE ECUMENICAL MOVEMENT: PAST, PRESENT, FUTURE
VOLOS, GREECE, 8-12 JUNE 2008

1. We offer thanks and glory to God for the inter-Orthodox consultation: "And many women were there..." (Mt. 27, 55) Participation of Orthodox Women in the Ecumenical Movement: Past, Present, Future, which was held on 8-12 June 2008 at the Volos Academy for Theological Studies, Greece. The meeting was sponsored by the programme for Women in Church and Society of the World Council of Churches (WCC) and hosted by the Diocese of Demetrias. The participants were welcomed by His Eminence Ignatios, Metropolitan of Demetrias and Almyros. Forty-five women from Eastern and Oriental Orthodox churches in Europe, Middle East, Asia, Australia and North America discussed the participation, ministry and concerns of Orthodox women in the church and in the ecumenical movement. Prominent women theologians and scholars offered a review of the history of the various meetings and consultations and of the major concerns expressed by Orthodox women over the past decades to promote women's participation in the various spheres of church life: liturgical, ministerial and administrative. Particular attention was given to the assessment of the present situation of women in their respective Orthodox churches, communities and ecumenical bodies.

2. The participants noted the important role that the WCC has played throughout the sixty years of its existence in promoting the concerns of women of all the member churches, including sponsoring consultations for Orthodox women. Many of these consultations held over the past thirty years were also supported by the leadership of the various Orthodox churches, e.g. Agapia, Romania (1976); Rhodes, Greece (1988); Crete, Greece (1990); Damascus, Syria (1996); and Istanbul, Turkey (1997). At these consultations a number of important

concerns relevant to the life of women in the church were expressed. We understand that the statements from these meetings represented the consensus of all the participants and summarized what they felt to be the important issues facing women in the church.

3. The participants noted with thanksgiving that the situation for Orthodox women in some contexts had reached significant milestones by the grace of God, including establishing a Special Synodical Commission on Women's Issues (Church of Greece), approving changes in language of occasional prayers concerning women (Holy Synod of Antioch), the blessing of deaconesses for ministry (Coptic Orthodox Church) participating in the decision-making process at the parish and church level, and serving as readers and choir leaders (Finland).

4. However, many of the concerns of women have not yet been fully addressed within the life of the church and are still relevant today. For instance:

a. a need for better access to and funding for Orthodox women to study theology and then, if desired, to have the opportunity for employment within the church;

b. a need to support pastoral care ministries by Orthodox women and to others (e.g., hospice, hospital, nursing home, prison and other institutional, community and military chaplaincies) and equip women for this ministry;

c. a need for women to be included in decision-making processes in the administrative bodies of their churches;

d. a need to address the understanding of women's biology and the dignity of women, including the prayers and practices associated with women's menstrual cycle, childbirth, 40-day churching, miscarriages etc.;

e. a yearning for women to be admitted into the "minor orders" (e.g., altar server, blessed reader, chanter etc.) and newer ministries (e.g., preacher) to more fully serve within the liturgical assembly and other ministries and to better serve the needs of women and men in the church;

f. a holy desire for the restoration of the order of deaconess and a rejuvenation of all diaconal work.

5. Since the last inter-Orthodox women's consultation in Istanbul,
Turkey in 1997, many changes have taken place both globally and lo-
cally in the Orthodox churches and their respective countries. Therefore, we feel a full assessment of the current situation and needs of
Orthodox women is required as well as development of a framework
for future action in order to identify areas of common concern as well
as differences and to provide an overview of the complexity of the
many current realities –social, cultural, economic, political– affecting
the life of Orthodox women.

Among the vehicles for assessing needs and responding to concerns could be:

a. convening general regional meetings of Orthodox women to address
not only our universal concerns but also many of those specific to
local situations, and to encourage mutual support and networking
to solve country/church-specific problems;

b. establishing a desk or focal point at the WCC for Orthodox women
that would follow up on the challenges identified and provide support for the involvement of women in various aspects of church
life, as well as safe space for discussion of sensitive issues;

c. supporting a website, and other existing internet resources, for
Orthodox women to accumulate theological materials, guides to
applied ministry etc., as well as provide a space for discussion fo-
rums;

d. encouraging theological research on issues of concern to women in
the life of the church.

6. We invite the WCC to continue this process in close cooperation and with full support of the Orthodox Church leadership. We
see the need to identify together with our church leadership the ways
and instruments to implement decisions and recommendations of
women's consultations in our churches. The implementation process
can be strengthened through involving Orthodox women appointed

as representatives of their churches or serving with the blessing of the church and other women of good faith.

7. We affirm that men and women, lay and ordained, belong to the overall Body of Christ. We recognize that these issues come through active engagement of all members. Therefore, we desire to promote dialogue by convening conferences for women and men (e.g., pastoral care, liturgical renewal etc.) to further deepen the faith of all Orthodox Christians.

8. The consultation was enriched by the contributions of the participants who shared their current experience of church ministry, such as women's involvement in

- ecumenical and inter-religious dialogue;
- revitalizing the life of the church and its social ministry, especially in Eastern Europe after the fall of communism;
- establishing national and global networks that promote theological research in women's issues, share information, and equip women for applied ministry; and
- establishing women's committees within church structures.

9. Women are called to holiness and ministry through baptism, and already serve the Body of Christ and his church through

- their witness and teaching;
- their intercession, advice and guidance as spiritual mothers;
- their dynamic evangelical ministry in all areas of pastoral and social work;
- their caring for the poor, ill and homeless;
- their offering prayer and comfort for those in need.

The conference participants encourage women in these ministries and call upon the WCC and its Orthodox member churches to consider seriously and implement the points of this report to strengthen the ecumenical participation and the ministries of Orthodox women, moving forward all together.

I. HISTORICAL AND THEOLOGICAL REFLECTION

ORTHODOX WOMEN IN THEOLOGICAL AND ECUMENICAL CONTEXT: ASSESSING CONCERNS FOR TODAY AND THE FUTURE (THE MORE THINGS SEEM TO CHANGE, THE MORE THEY STAY THE SAME?)

KYRIAKI KARIDOYANES-FITZGERALD

INTRODUCTION

We are here today as a result of the sacrifice made over many years, by many, many persons, far too numerous to mention now; persons who have labored to establish and maintain the World Council of Churches (WCC). Many of these persons are Orthodox. Others are non-Orthodox Christians, who fervently desire authentic unity among Christians (and peace throughout the world!) and who have extended themselves in service to us and to courageous multilateral dialogue through the agency of the WCC. Informed and thoughtful Orthodox men and women are deeply indebted to these efforts. Lessons learned and constructive critical observations to be expressed here –as well as newly born initiatives, fledgling and tentative as these may be– would not have begun without this remarkable foundation. This is a foundation that comprises prayer, investment of human and financial recourses, trustworthy research and courageous interpersonal engagement. It is vital to recall this original foundation, as I identify what I observe to be historic successes as well as challenges and failures of this effort conducted by both the WCC and by Orthodox themselves on behalf of Orthodox women.

The issue of Orthodox women in ministry is a vital one for the church, as in the end this effects all Orthodox Christians, male and female. Speaking only for myself, I have come to believe that the assumption of some who relegate the importance of discerning women's ministries as a separate issue –even perhaps as "optional" or an "interesting addendum" or as "less important" to the life, witness, mission and work of the Orthodox Church– is tantamount to sin, as even "when one member suffers, all members suffer".

Today's programme announces the general theme to be "Re-Capturing the Past". As I understood the invitation that was extended to me and which I accepted, I am to present this honourable audience with a synopsis of the most important lessons I have learned from my past experience regarding the progress of the ministries of women in the Orthodox Church in ecumenical context and concerns for the future. I will keep five important Orthodox meetings especially in mind having to do with the participation of women in the life of the Orthodox Church which have taken place since the mid-1970s. These are Agapia, 1976; Rhodes, 1988; Crete, 1990; Damascus, 1996; and Istanbul (Constantinople), 1997.

Nevertheless, please understand that while I am here to highlight some of the most important lessons I have learned through these past thirty years, I am here specifically not to "re-capture the past" with you (*alemonon mas!*). This is because I think that the fundamental problem today for faithful Orthodox women in theology serving in an ecumenical context is that, at least since the 1970s, we are caught in a trap of an imbalanced and repeating cycle of "re-capturing the past". But which view of the past, and what or who does any particular rendition of the past serve? I don't know with any certainty. Still, perhaps the most painful lesson I have learned while reviewing this past occurred in large part through bearing embarrassed witness to the regurgitation of repeated themes and dynamics, over and over and over again, with precious little progress in applying "orthopraxia".

While regurgitation may be healthy for certain animals, it is not healthy for humans! Regurgitation offers no true life for human persons! The regurgitation with regard to women's concerns may actually reflect fallen human objectives and not those of the church. This critical observation calls to mind the Lord's question: "What does it profit to gain the whole world and lose one's own soul?" All of our activities are called to be theocentric and based in love for the "other" in the presence of God. When considering this more thoughtfully, we realize this entails a huge risk. Nevertheless, the Lord's "greatest commandment" prods us to take these risks, all the while looking to him: "You shall love the Lord your God with all of your heart and all of your soul and with all of your mind"... and... "You shall love your neighbour as yourself".

TRUE PRIORITIES: DISCERNING AN ORTHODOX THEOLOGICAL APPROACH TO CONTEMPORARY CHALLENGES

Every Christian is called in his or her own way to bear anew their witness to the "one thing necessary". This calls to mind the "approach" of the Church, which is "for the life of the world". And this approach is always fresh, as it is authentic, where through the life of the Holy Spirit in the Church, Jesus Christ is ever-present; and it is three-fold: 1) doxological, 2) pastoral and 3) relational.

a. Doxological. The Orthodox consider doxology to be the highest expression of theology. An approach that is doxological must be at the heart of every effort we conduct on behalf of the Church; including those related to the participation of women in the life of the Church! We must carefully bear in mind, however, that genuine doxology is not an exercise in arrogant triumphalism (*alemonon mas!*). Rather, it is the end-point of our life's journey toward God. This end-point, through the loving activity of the Holy Spirit, is fully present with us now, where we are called to surrender every moment in the present to the embrace of the Lord's astounding and infinite love, He who is the Alpha and Omega. This foundation of trusting, unconditional loving surrender and praise becomes the prayer undergirding every initiative within the life of the Church, including initiatives regarding women! In everyday practice, this sets before us the quiet unending discipline of our radical listening and surrender so as to receive the loving God himself through his ineffable mercy. In this way, we may offer selfless praise and thanksgiving to the only One who is truly holy. This serves as the foundation of every action conducted in the name of the Lord.

b. Pastoral. Secondly, such an approach must be pastoral. By "pastoral", I imply that we are the "reason-endowed sheep" following after the one and true Great Shepherd, He who is the Author of life. From this perspective, approaches that are genuinely pastoral bear witness to and give life; this includes initiatives that concern Orthodox women. To quote from class notes of a beloved former dogmatic theology professor of mine from the School of Theology of Thessaloniki, "In order for dogmatic theology to be real, it must be pastoral, as true theology always heals and gives life". True theology makes way for the loving energies of God to bring us and all of creation ever closer to Him. The fruits of the genuinely pastoral include forgiveness, reconciliation, healing, healthy change, growth, unity, renewal and transformation/ sanctification. We must carefully pay attention here that all of these fruits are essentially relational, thus further promoting authentic (i.e., life-giving) relationships.

c. Relational. Thirdly, such an approach must be relational, as we worship the merciful, loving God who ineffably abides in Three-in-One relationship, in whose "image ad likeness" we have been created. This third foundation in some ways reflects the same discipline required of doxology, as human persons are called to i) listen and discern, ii) surrender to and iii) receive one another as they engage in relationship; this includes initiatives concerning women. Such an effort requires our setting aside of fallen ego attachments. This is how we find our true selves: by risking the loss of our life as we know it for the life of the other. To be in authentic relationship with anyone in the presence of the loving God implies that we are always willing to be forever changed at a moment's notice. This discipline directs us away from fallen self-centredness and toward cultivating authentic relationships: in other words, toward communion (*koinonia*) with the thrice-holy God, our own selves, one another and creation.

This very rough sketch[1] strives to bear witness to the approach of

---

1. I have discussed this more fully in my book *Persons in Communion: A Theology of Authentic Relationships*, Patriarch Athenagoras Orthodox Institute, Berkeley, CA, 2006.

the Church and be expressed through the various contexts of life today, including the new challenges regarding the participation of wom-
en in the life of the Church. Yes, this approach generally may be less
provocatively antagonistic and polarizing (i.e., "political") than the
fallen world's perspective. The Church is called to serve "the politics
of God" on earth ("Your Kingdom come, Your will be done on earth
as it is in heaven") rather than the politics of fallen man. The main difference between this and other approaches is that the will of the living
God of love is given its full due, with no "yes, buts . . . ". Of course,
this objective is impossible for fallen human beings, but "what is impossible for man is possible with God". This approach helps cultivate
souls, hearts and minds (including our own), while humbly seeking
the mercy of the Lord and the discernment of the Holy Spirit, in order
to prioritize engaging in the spiritual warfare of our times.

THEME AND VARIATIONS SINCE THE 1970s

Reviewing the conclusions from the Orthodox international conferences and consultations on the participation of women in the life of
the Church (Agapia, 1976; Rhodes, 1988; Crete, 1990; Damascus,
1996; Istanbul, 1997) will quickly make the reader realize that many
of the major themes, concerns and suggestions have been repeated
over and over again throughout these and other meetings.

Please note that the formats of these meetings varied in important, yet mutually related ways. For example on the one hand, the
WCC-sponsored meetings held in Agapia (1976) and Crete (1990)
could be considered international "focus" or "study" type groups.
Focus groups are used by profit and not-for-profit corporations to
break new ground and prioritize important concerns that are to be
addressed by a larger body of people. Focus group work occurs *before*
updated or new information is taken to a wider audience for further
deliberation and potential action. Focus groups are very important
vehicles in helping discern new ways of conducting business or life
within a larger group. The final authority, however, never resides with

a focus group. "Authority" ultimately abides with the officials and other representatives formally recognized and trusted as such to represent the interests of the larger group.

On the other hand, the 1988 Rhodes, Greece consultation was not a focus group type of gathering, but rather this meeting made good use of the work previously conducted. The Rhodes consultation is perhaps the most official and authoritative meeting regarding Orthodox women of our time. Every Orthodox Autocephalous Church was invited by the Ecumenical Patriarchate of Constantinople under the leadership of the late patriarch, His All Holiness Patriarch Demetrios, to send official hierarchal representation to this historic event. In addition to this, numerous theologians were invited to participate in the deliberations. A third of the participants were women theologians, some of whom were nuns from various monasteries, others were married or single and living in the world, and still other theologians were wives of Orthodox clergy. The conclusions of this consultation vigorously affirmed the previous work conducted by the Orthodox, including the work in Agapia. An enthusiastic and "unanimous" call for the rejuvenation of women ordained to the diaconate, in those places where this ministry may be needed, also was expressed powerfully. The Rhodes conclusions were enthusiastically affirmed and elaborated upon at a subsequent WCC-sponsored Orthodox women's consultation held in Crete, 1990.

The Damascus, Syria (October 1996) and Istanbul (May 1997) meetings were also unique events in the life of the Orthodox Church. These too were not "focus groups" of preparatory study and discussion. Rather, they were conducted as "one event in two locations" in order to hear the voices of Orthodox women internationally.

The regional Orthodox churches from the Middle East, Australia, Asia and Africa were invited to send representatives to the Damascus meeting; while the regional Orthodox churches from Eastern and Western Europe, North and South America were invited to send representatives to the meeting in Istanbul, Turkey. This meeting also had a special authority, as the women who were invited, except for a small number of persons who served as consultants or were sent at the invitation of the WCC, did not simply make up a group of self-selected friends, or professional or political allies advocating for a specific predetermined, self-serving objective. The women delegates who were invited were discerned and chosen by their own regional and local churches and sent as official representatives. As the Orthodox theological coordinator of these events, I can bear witness that no one from my office had any knowledge or direct influence regarding who the churches would send to represent them. We anticipated a variety of women, and indeed this is what the churches sent. Moreover, except for striving to facilitate discussions fairly and in a manner that would benefit the group at large, there were absolutely no behind-the-scene arrangements made prior to or during these events by my office that would be considered self-serving and/or manipulative of the discussion process[2]. Looking back today and bearing all of the above in mind, it is amazing how this diverse group, of their own accord, powerfully expressed concerns that echoed back to the 1970s, all the way back to Agapia.

In summary, the repeated concerns raised over the decades are understood less in terms of theology and more in terms of better applying "orthopraxia". These concerns address many dimensions of Christian life and vocation, not merely ordination per se. They are the following:

Christ is Risen. Nothing can separate us from the loving God who loved us first. Through every expression of adult Christian life –monastic, married, single or widowed– the Lord calls each of his friends who have "put on Christ" through baptism to ever strive to "be renewed in the spirit of your mind" and to "put on the new person"

---

2. Furthermore, there were no discussions prior to or during these events that unfairly benefitted any one particular person or special interest group for financial or for other opportunistic reasons.

through the daily relationships, responsibilities, challenges and opportunities presented to us. This affirmation is at the heart of Orthodox Christian faith for men and women. Women attending these conferences clearly identify themselves as faithful and full members of the Church.

Since the 1970s, Orthodox Christians around the world have survived (and many still continue to bear) various types of political, economic and religious difficulties, even oppression. Despite these offensive distractions and this suffering, throughout the past three decades the Orthodox have continued to affirm with conviction that "Christ is in our midst". Women in particular have been courageously extending themselves as "peacemakers" (Mt. 5:9) in their local contexts. Furthermore, women have been active in local, regional and national philanthropy and social welfare. These types of initiatives are to be recognized, appreciated, supported and wherever possible, increased through the life of the church, as they demonstrate obedience to the Lord's directive to us to "love your neighbor as you love yourself". Recognizing and supporting the numerous ministries within the laity, the "royal priesthood", to which men and women may be called has been stressed extensively. In some contexts, there are numerous ministries within the "royal priesthood" exhibited by Orthodox women (and men) which present a vibrant witness to the "variety of gifts" of the Holy Spirit offered within the life of the Church for the common good. Since the 1970s, many conferences and meetings have strongly urged that this vibrant witness be further cultivated. Furthermore, there was a repeated emphasis for women's involvement and participation in the everyday decision-making process of their local churches.

Sadly, the above vibrant witness is not true for every context. At more than one meeting, the following statements by women delegates and participants was heard, officially and unofficially, with a profound note of pain: "women are more easily expendable", they are "easily dismissed". The delegates even asked for help in addressing this by requesting: i) more opportunities to meet with Orthodox women (Eastern Orthodox together with Oriental Orthodox) in order to continue building these efforts; ii) increased opportunities for ecumenical contact and witness (e.g., asking for more female representatives to participate at the 1998 WCC assembly meeting in Harare); iii) aid in disseminating their conclusions throughout the world. Looking toward the WCC, they even requested a resource centre be established to help manage this effort.

Orthodox women fervently desire an immediate increase in opportunities for pastoral care be extended to them, especially by other faithful women who are theologically, spiritually and pastorally prepared to undertake these expressions of ministry.

Orthodox women value highly Orthodox Christian theology, teaching and the "*phronema*" of the Church. Their responsibilities within the community and especially within the family oblige them to serve as primary educators. Orthodox women desire more opportunities in theological education, both formally (by encouraging women to study at Orthodox theological schools and, once there, by making it easier for them to attend) and informally (through other types of opportunities in order to better reach women in their context).

Cultural assumptions about the "ritual uncleanliness" and capacities of women that hinder discerning more clearly their participation within the life of the church community must be re-examined and corrected to better bear witness to Orthodox Christian teaching.

Clergy wives must be more thoughtfully appreciated and supported in the various ways and contexts through which they participate in the life of the Church. In addition to the pressures of everyday life, dedicated service within the life of the church presents extra challenges and opportunities to clergy families. Furthermore, monasticism and ministries in "minor orders", as well as new expressions of service and ministry within the life of the church, need to be seriously considered, wherever discerned necessary and appropriate.

Since the first meeting in Agapia, while affirming Orthodox scholarship dating back to the 1940s, the rejuvenation of women ordained to the diaconate or "deaconesses" has been repeatedly affirmed at various meetings and conferences as another potentially vital expression of ministry within the life of the Church for those contexts where they may be needed. It must be noted here that the ministry of deaconesses has survived in a few places, even to our own day. In more recent years, the Church of Greece in 2004 re-affirmed its commitment to the rejuvenation of the ministry of deaconesses as already expressed in the canons, at least wherever needed in Orthodox monasteries[3]. Despite there being numerous expressions of encouragement since the 1970s to pursue the rejuvenation of this order of ministry in those places where it may be needed, only one other response addressed this officially in recent years. These deliberations occurred as part of the October 2006 Standing Conference of Canonical Orthodox Bishops in the Americas (SCOBA), held in Chicago, Illinois[4]. Furthermore, I am also personally aware of active, yet discreet, initiatives both in the Eastern Orthodox "old" and "new" worlds advocating for the rejuvenation of this ministry. From my perspective, we are not hindered from taking this step for lack of spiritual need or discerning bishops, clergy, theologians and communities; nor for the lack of existing trustworthy, mature and pastorally competent possible candidates. Except for the two historic meetings of the Church of Greece in 2004 and SCOBA in 2006, I do not know of any further significant official developments since the 1996 Damascus and 1997 Istanbul meetings that have directly addressed these concerns. The ordination of women to the presbyterate and episcopacy was a topic that was not aggressively examined in the official discussions at any of the aforementioned conferences. Nevertheless, the delegates at the Istanbul meeting *on their*

3. See: http://old.orthodoxnews.org
4. See: "http://www.scoba.us/statements/2006-10-06-spiritual-moral-concerns. html; "http://www.scoba.us/resources/2006conference.html?mp4=deaconate.mp4; and "http://www.orthodoxwomen.org/files/SCOBA_Women_Deacons.pdf".

own time did invite Prof. Constantine Yiokarinis to present his findings on this issue. This may indicate that while Orthodox women may not believe this to be a calling for women, they are not afraid to listen to others or to consider and discuss this topic. Prof. Yiokarinis also reported on the deliberations and conclusions of the International Orthodox and Old Catholic Bilateral Theological Dialogue, which explored this issue in 1996 and 1997. These historic conclusions have been published in Greek, German and English[5].

By the 1997 Istanbul meeting, it had become clear to the delegates attending at that time that, once again, themes being discussed and issues being raised echoed back to the 1970s. Openly afraid of the "circular file" (i.e., the waste basket), these delegates expressed a specific and heartfelt plea to the WCC to help disseminate these findings throughout the Orthodox world, both to ordained and lay leadership, as well as the rest of the faithful. This request may have been a historic step for Orthodox women representatives expressing their voice, making clear what they needed to others who professed to be friends and benefactors: that the prayer, study and dialogue of many years must be acknowledged and responded to with appropriate and swift action.

CONCERNS FOR MOVING FORWARD: SAFETY

In order to discuss and discern better how to proceed from here, "safety" must be considered at this time. Safety has been an important word used by organizers of every WCC meeting concerning women I have ever attended. Even today, our deliberations and private discus-

---

5. These meetings are historic in that, while not advocating for this to occur, at least at an informal, yet official and professional theological level, for the first time a delegation of Orthodox theologians could not find a reason for prohibiting the ordination of women to these orders of ministry. See: Urs von Arx & Anastasios Kallis (eds.), "Gender and the Image of Christ", Duncan Reid, trans, *Anglican Theological Review* 84.3 (2002), p. 485-755.

sions must respect all of the participants involved, and this includes respecting their safety. But what kind of responsibility does this really imply? Do we (WCC and others) really know what it means to build a safe environment for deliberation of a sensitive topic with a vulnerable population?

Over the course of many years, in addition to my vocation in Orthodox theology, I have learned much through my occupation as a professional health service provider, licensed to practice independently in psychology where I live in the United States. During this time period, I have developed a specialization of working with female and male survivors from various types of trauma, abuse and addictions, including sexual abuse, physical abuse, psychological abuse (which includes intimidation) and financial abuse. For trauma survivors to begin to experience healing, as well as to subsequently flourish, safety is the first and last concern.

In my work with every person who comes to see me in my office, but especially with trauma survivors, there are three interdependent aspects of safety to which, I, as the caregiver and/or benefactor, must be accountable at all times. Safety is always a living issue. In order to promote safety in our ecumenical context, these same principles must also be respected fully; otherwise, the exchange is less than authentic:

Establishing fundamental safety. This obliges the caregiver or benefactor to provide the foundation needed for the survivor to freely and peacefully express her or his experiences and ideas, painful or difficult as these may be, without the fear of reprisal. This includes safety from physical, professional, financial and psychological acts of punishment for sharing the secret with others. The burden of responsibility for preparing and maintaining such a safe context is with the benefactor or care-giver – *not the survivor of the abuse!*

Freedom to enjoy trustworthiness. This concerns confidentiality and fair play. First, confidences must be respected and maintained only with those who have been clearly designated to receive the privileged information. Trustworthiness also includes being open when exceptions are to be made regarding confidentiality. Second, fair play concerns treating each vulnerable person or population to be engaged with equal respect and fair-mindedness by carefully avoiding the temptation of unduly predetermining the course of discussion toward any specific person's or subgroup's favor. Whenever such prearranged and often "secret" proceedings occur, the container for safety is contaminated from the very start. The burden of responsibility for preparing and maintaining such a safe context is with the benefactor or care-giver – *not the survivors of the abuse!*

Timely and honest advocacy. This concerns well-timed and straightforward support by care-givers and/or benefactors in respectful collaboration with the survivors. Sadly, attempts at advocacy fail too often at this stage. This usually occurs when the benefactor informs the person they are trying to help how to feel and what he or she needs. At this phase of the relationship, survivors of abuse risk being re-traumatized, as this kind of false assistance is like survivors mustering up the courage to ask for an apple and instead being given a banana, sometimes with an added comment like, "This, is what you really need". Once again, even here the burden of responsibility for preparing and maintaining such a safe context is more with the benefactor or care-giver – *not the survivors of the abuse!*

With these above safety concerns and developments since the 1998 WCC Harare assembly in mind, I have very serious reservations regarding how safety will be implemented from this point forward.

CONCLUSIONS: BY THEIR FRUITS YOU WILL KNOW THEM

As we begin our conclusions, let us consider how we must strive to remember that we are not, nor have we ever been, alone. We must continue to strive trusting and re-affirming the ancient adage, "One Christian is no Christian". While, sadly, some from among us may have been obliged to bear extra heavy and indescribable burdens as a result of witnessing to the gospel regarding the many ways God calls women and men to serve Him, we must affirm the fact that none of us are, nor ever have been, completely alone. Our Lord assures his friends and followers of this in the gospel of St. Matthew, declaring that "'I am with you always, even unto the end of the world'".

As baptized members of God's Church, we affirm that the source of this mystery abides within us, among us and around us, as much as He is beyond us. This assertion is based in the life of the Holy Spirit who still abides in the Church. It is the Holy Spirit who points us to Christ, and makes Him present to us in ways we cannot fathom. By "having put on Christ" this way, we are intimately and mysteriously united to Him and to all of those who are in Him—our brothers and sisters whom we see and the holy ones of God, the saints and heavenly hosts who are present yet invisible to our physical eyes.

In practical terms, what does this really mean, to become holy, one with God and his saints? Perhaps, we can be inspired by the example set before us through considering the enigmatic hologram. Science informs us that holograms in nature contain within themselves the complete "mystery", the entirety or fullness of an organism's or substance's composition through to its tiniest fraction. This is true even if this smallest portion is invisible to the human eye. For any and every ministry within the life of the Church to be truly life-giving in its fullness today, Orthodox women (and men!) must become a living "hologram" of the same life-giving witness expressed by of the holy women (and men!) of the Church throughout the ages – as we have all been intimately "knit together" into one body. And so our discipline must be doxological, pastoral and relational, somehow making present in a mysterious way the life of the church. Surely, yes, this is impossible. Yet, what is impossible for us is possible with God, and we wait for his love, direction and help.

Our Lord asks his followers, "What does it profit a person to gain the whole world and lose one's own soul?" Analyses of power dynamics in themselves, while sometimes very necessary and helpful in identifying sin, never have "saved" persons on their own terms. They never have, nor ever will! Scrupulous analyses of power dynamics, be they "echoes" of various feminist or anti-feminist biases and agendas, do not save per se – ever!

All too often, the very activity of scrupulous analysis takes on a life of its own, thus creating its own universe, distracting the researcher from the "one thing necessary". Sadly, it seems to me that a "mini-universe" has been created over the decades in association with the WCC, which has not been serving the needs of Orthodox women effectively. For example, when our witness and voices identified priorities and made specific requests, as exemplified in particular through the statements of the delegates attending the Damascus and Constantinople Orthodox women's conferences, other projects and agendas were later offered instead to "help" us (more bananas!). Some of these would be very nice to enjoy (in fact, I very much like bananas), but honestly, is this the way to use the precious, currently dwindling WCC resources allotted for such a task?

It appears as if other, far more pressing, issues expressed by Orthodox women delegates themselves have been addressed only superficially, or perhaps more accurately may have been outright ignored and replaced by others. With the dramatic changes that have taken place over the past decade, it is imperative to examine, identify, acknowledge and make corrective course responses. To "move on" without an honest evaluation as to how well priorities were identified, resources were spent and follow-through occurred courts future failure. Would any one of us choose to invest our hard earned money and other resources in ventures that did not conduct such a thorough self-appraisal? Scientific, and especially psychological, research methodology affirms that: inherited problems which are not fully acknowledged in both organizational structure and inter-personal human process, cannot be confronted and healed... We undermine our own future selves by avoiding this challenge.

With the above in mind, the most important issues that need to be addressed decisively resulting from these past efforts all concern "*orthopraxia*". They include,

- implementing more avenues for Orthodox women to learn from one another on our own terms as Orthodox;
- aggressively promoting theological education for Orthodox women;
- actively supporting the development of officially sanctioned ministries in pastoral care for women to be conducted by Orthodox women;
- supporting the ministry of clergy wives and the spiritual witness of monastics;
- exploring the possibilities of "minor orders" for women, as well as the development of new ministries;
- rejuvenating the ministry of the deaconess in those places where it is needed; and
- addressing perhaps the most flagrant disappointment of all – that is, the disregard of the specific heartfelt plea to the WCC to disseminate these findings throughout the Orthodox world, both to ordained and lay leadership, as well as the rest of the faithful.

As identified earlier, conference after conference, meeting after meeting seem to be regurgitating over and over again the same list of "a theme and variations" for the application of *orthopraxia* regarding the participation of women in the Orthodox Church. It is important to note here that as Orthodox women we deeply appreciate that healthy change often comes slowly. Nevertheless, since the 1970s, with the exception of a few grassroots initiatives, there seems to have been only minimal investment in a more authentic application of *orthopraxia* regarding Orthodox women's issues. To continue in this manner insults faithful Orthodox women and men; and furthermore, it is abusive.

In clinical psychology there is a popular saying amongst scientists conducting research that tempts me to fear for the future: "The best predictor of future performance is past behavior". In all sincerity, allow me today to ask the WCC to re-examine honestly and thoroughly its relationship with Orthodox women before it proceeds to exhaust remaining allocated resources any further. God-willing, as the WCC begins to honestly re-examine its effectiveness in extending assistance to Orthodox Christian women, I believe that Orthodox women and men, while offering support to this effort as they can, need not wait around passively for their conclusions.

We can begin to address and build on the important affirmations made since the 1970s in fresh ways, ways that are of the church: doxological, pastoral and relational. Already there are a number of wonderful Orthodox women's groups that have been formed in North America that include a concern for education, and that have to varying degrees a theological and/or spiritual focus. I wish to briefly identify St. Catherine's Vision, a group I know most about, to share as an example with you.

ST. CATHERINE'S VISION

About eight years ago, a small group of Orthodox women theologians and a few highly trustworthy friends from various Orthodox jurisdictions together began to communicate with one another in order to discern how to more faithfully address the concerns raised through the previously identified conferences. As a result of these discussions, two retreats for women graduates of Orthodox theological schools (2005, 2007)[6] took place, as well as the publication of a new kind of creative study on women saints entitled *Encountering Women of Faith*. With very little financial assistance, and through much, much investment of time through intimate community-building both within our group and outside of it, St. Catherine's Vision (SCV) was established.

SCV is the only pan-Orthodox organization of its kind endorsed by SCOBA. Reflecting carefully upon the findings repeatedly expressed through the efforts of the conferences in Romania (1976); Rhodes, Greece (1988); Crete, Greece (1990); Damascus (1996); Istanbul/Constantinople (1997) and elsewhere, our working group is committed to

6. See: "http://www.orthodoxwomen.org".

contributing to the mission of the Church through initiatives that address three inter-related objectives. These are: spiritual renewal, unity, and education.

SCV offers a small example of what Orthodox women faithfully working together as a community of sisters over the course of several years may accomplish with next to no infrastructure, no spare time, little spare energy and few financial resources. Together, we engage one another in a "discipline of Love, seeking the discernment of the Holy Spirit", as we allow ourselves to be crucified through deeply listening to one another at a pace that is, sometimes, slower than molasses. True listening, we find, is an important askesis of today. Nevertheless, life-giving changes have been quietly occurring for a number of persons who have been closely working with us through the years as a result –at least in part– of this effort. Still, this work requires ongoing faith, courage and humble perseverance. Surely up to this point, this path has been a long and rocky uphill climb. Nevertheless, while young and fragile, SCV is still growing, as together we strive to "hear the word of God and keep it"! There are two other SCV board members taking part in this conference, one of whom will be offering you a better overview of who we are later in the program.

I wish to end with the following words of St. Nicholas Cabasilas, as they remind me of what we strive to remember as we proceed with our initiative through SCV. His words may be just as true with every endeavor initiated on behalf of Orthodox Christianity and Christians everywhere. He writes,

> Christ gives to human persons life and growth, nourishment and light and breath. He opens their eyes and gives them light and the power to see. He gives to human persons the bread of life, and this bread is nothing else than himself, He is life for those who breathe. He clothes those who desire to be clothed. He strengthens the traveler and He is the way. He is at once both the inn along the road and the destination of the journey.

When we struggle, He struggles at our side. When we argue, He is the arbiter. And when we win the victory, He is the prize[7].

7. *The Life in Christ*, 1.1.

"MANY WOMEN WERE ALSO THERE..." – EVEN INTO THE 21ST CENTURY: REFLECTION ON THE PAST SIXTY YEARS OF ORTHODOX WOMEN IN WCC AND THE ECUMENICAL MOVEMENT

LEONIE LIVERIS

INTRODUCTION

It is with great pleasure that I find myself once again in the presence of so many Orthodox women who share a dream of their empowerment for ministry and gender justice in the Church and in society. It would be remiss of me not to express at the outset my thanks to the World Council of Church's (WCC) women's programme and the Volos Academy for Theological Studies for providing this unique and special opportunity to meet and the invitation to myself to share with you a brief overview of the contemporary history of Orthodox women in the ecumenical movement and in their churches. I believe we have a duty to know our ecumenical past when much was said and written and achieved during the 20th century. This is a time to speak openly with honesty and forthrightness of our hopes for the future. And we can do this while carrying forward the work of Orthodox pioneers of this modern era –both women and men– who have provided us with new ways of reading scripture, new ways of researching history, and of writing and expressing Orthodox theology. These new ways are revealed through our research in the archives, the stories that have been hidden of extraordinary Orthodox women – saints, martyrs and unknown faithful witnesses. My address comes from my long time research and involvement in the ecumenical movement.

It is important that we start with the understanding there is no point in reinventing the wheel or merely repeating past work. Since 1948, many recommendations have emerged out of many consultations, and for some here present, we have in our different ways endeavoured to carry forward the inspiring and challenging hopes from various meetings and seminars. I make it clear from the outset that the focus of my professional studies, qualifications and work has been as a social and feminist historian. I have not completed a theological degree, and my research and comments in this address will perhaps come from a different perspective than some of my learned sisters.

We delegates have been invited by the organizers to be challenged to explore not only the ways in which we can empower ourselves, but how we can reach out to all women in local and ecumenical contexts. In this way, we can contribute to overcoming human barriers and divisions within our Orthodox Church life, expanding to embrace all women. We have not only to plan for our radical service but also to be self-critical in areas where revelation may be painful and confronting. For too long we have been tentative and nervous about expressing our deepest concerns and sense of disenfranchisement as laity in the proper order of the church. Do we have the courage of our inner convictions to bring to our church hierarchy a stark and honest assessment of where we are and where we hope to be?

The insightful and direct words of a 19th-century Christian woman are a constant reminder of how much we need to seriously ask what have we achieved, one what has stopped our work. In 1893 Matilda Joslyn Gage wrote in her seminal work *Women, Church and the State* that

> women of the present century… who struggle for equal opportunity for education with men; for a chance to enter the liberal professions; for a fair share of the world of work; for equal pay for that work; for all the demands of equality which make this a noted age in world history; have met their greatest opposition from the Church… For it has robbed woman of her responsibility, putting man in place of God, forbidden her the offices of the Church… and denied her independent thought declaring her a secondary creation to man[1].

1. Matilda Joslyn Gage, *Woman, Church and State* [1893], Ayer Books, Salem MA, 1980, p. 525.

So how do we move forward and challenge ourselves for the future? For many Orthodox laity, their meaningful engagement within the ecumenical movement has served two purposes. First, it has assisted in revealing to other Christians the Orthodox faith's complexity and rich history; the culture and tradition of its people; both its conservatism and its intransigence to change; and its beauty and awesome tradition. Second, and more importantly, ecumenism has served to deepen and enrich the often scattered and erratic understanding many Orthodox themselves have of their own church. The oft-heard criticisms that somehow even the notion of ecumenism itself is antithetical to Orthodox belief is in my view a defensive opinion of those who do not wish to open themselves to the world at large, preferring to turn inward and adopt, to my mind, an un-Christian and self-righteous antagonism to all who are not Orthodox. I believe that the many who have tentatively ventured into the ecumenical unknown have enriched their Christian faith and in turn enriched others in understanding our Orthodox Church, its theology, Tradition and culture.

There are a few women and men in the Orthodox Church who have lived as the "other" in the Church universal, and our familial and cultural tradition has not been Greek or Russian or Coptic or Romanian or any other cultural or national Orthodox Church. Whether in the end this slants a bias of criticism or can indeed cause one to willingly surrender the "other" identity is an intriguing and baffling question that still requires much research. I raise a concern at this point that we can perhaps develop in our discussions. The growing fundamentalism amongst many converts –especially in the West, but also among the re-emerging believers in East– has, I believe, the potential of dragging the Orthodox Church back into a fearful, bigoted and inward perception of faith, one that embraces only the terrible punishment of the cross rather than the joyful and celebratory vision of the resurrection. Conservatism certainly has a place to preserve the Tradition that is indeed holy; but radical thinking and action is needed to truly respond to the liberating message of the scriptures. We need to be vigilant, not only from without but also from within. It is regrettable that, especially in the Diaspora in the West, disenchanted Anglicans (because of women priests) and Evangelical Protestants see the Orthodox Church as a place of stability and militant conservatism. New "believers" adapt their perception of the "old and pure" ways of being the church of past centuries, where Orthodoxy focused for example on how women behave, insisted on blind obedience to canon law, and enforced the authority and headship of husbands and fathers. Because of their devoutness and unquestioning adherence to the often archaic past, their influence with bishops and clergy is sometimes detrimental to others who in many ways have moved and on and into the 21st century.

We continue to work within the parameters determined by the church, and it is a brave person to speak and say that our faith calls us to witness and to challenge far more than we have to this time. As we work together towards a proposed future programme of action and involvement to take away with us, may I offer a note of caution as expressed at a consultation in Nicaragua in 1970: "a polite list of recommendations and resolutions can be a swindle, a hoax on both the participants and for the Church itself. They can give one a feeling that we accomplished something really vital". In reality we have decided on such a limited consensus of ideas, that our passion, challenges, innovative and critical analysis are lost, and we offer only a list for the wastepaper basket. We need to leave this meeting with radical and visionary ideals to share with those back in our own jurisdictions and parishes. We need recommendations that will inspire those not here with us to become passionate and moved to action, to feel that their estrangement from Church, as we sometimes feel ourselves, is a problem and that something must be done.

The structures of our churches and communities and ministries have become ends in themselves, seemingly inviolate and out of bounds with regard to change. We have structures that are answering problems that no longer exist, while ignoring the real needs of our community, both local and global. When we are less true to ourselves, we overcompensate the niceties so as not to offend, but as a result we are not being heard or acknowledged. Our obsequiousness in the traditional practice of obedience and politeness needs an overhaul – we need to stand up from our knees, straighten our back and raise our heads. We must be willing to take risks and be strong when we fail. Remember, men, both clergy and laity, have taken their authority for granted over centuries. They may stumble, fail, betray and fall in disgrace, and yet they keep going, always assuming their authority is a given right, not to be questioned.

THE EARLY YEARS: ORTHODOX WOMEN AND ECUMENICAL SISTERS

It is important to reflect on where we have been over the past sixty years, and why we are once again questioning and exploring our place in the ecumenical movement and our relationship with each other and the various families of the whole Orthodox Church. Our history is not easy; it is at times fraught with considerable angst and high-handedness. We have on many occasions been quick to claim a victim status in our relationships and slow to respond to the openness of spirit when offered by others.

When the WCC was founded in 1948, Prof. Lev Zander, Orthodox theologian in Paris, reflected that

> an early pronouncement against ecumenism by the Orthodox was an expression of ecclesiastical self-assertion, provincialism and suspicion – this provincialism was a disease of the spirit, that could attack all churches whatever their power, greatness or holiness[2].

We can certainly claim a lack of understanding on the part of other member churches, and their impatience with our steadfastness to history and tradition. Additionally, from all sides, from both individuals and communities, there has often been a display of personal antagonism

---

2. Lev Zander, "The Ecumenical Movement and the Orthodox Church", *The Ecumenical Review* 1.3 (1949), p. 12.

that does not bode well for a fully engaged Christian relationship. Having said all that, I now move to revisit the past with our contemporary ecumenical history of Orthodox women from 1947 focusing largely on my research of the WCC archives through my extended involvement in the ecumenical movement in Australia for over twenty years.

The contemporary history of women in the Eastern and Oriental Orthodox churches differs markedly from the emergence of women in the Catholic and Protestant communions of churches, which reflects the divisive history of the West. Scholars have written tomes on our history from all our traditions. However I do not intend to re-visit that troubled past beyond noting that I will focus my remarks towards a breaking of the cultural assumptions that have inhibited and silenced women through the centuries into a submission for some perceived greater good. Instead, I prefer to reveal the beginnings, when courageous women started a journey through their participation in the ecumenical movement.

The years following the second world war was a time of great sadness, loss and questioning of faith for many people. It was a time that left many of our families bereft of husbands, fathers and sons and a place of identity and belonging. Conscious of this great loss and in recognition of the incredible work undertaken by women during those years, the WCC was founded 1948 and based on the past efforts of the League of Nations after the first world war. In almost its first ecumenical programme before the first assembly, the WCC commissioned a worldwide study on how women had been fulfilling their roles in the churches, what women were now doing in church and society, and what they intended or wished to do in the future – and, importantly, whether their service would be in the church. The study included many of the Orthodox churches, noting that it was not until 1961 that all Orthodox churches were members of WCC.

In 1947, the study "The Life and Work of Women in the Church" was commissioned. The questionnaire was translated and sent to key women's organizations in over fifty countries and finally completed over a two-year period. In 1948, the interim report was presented in Amsterdam to the first WCC assembly by Sarah Chakko, an Orthodox woman from the Malankara Syrian Orthodox Church in India. Detailed and enlightening responses were received from Orthodox churches in Greece, Egypt, and Palestine; the Russian Orthodox community in France; the Coptic Church in Egypt; and the Armenian Apostolic Church in Lebanon. The most interesting and important observation concerning the questionnaires was that it was promoted not by the hierarchs of the church, but by committed churchwomen who were leaders in ecumenical organizations in their own countries. It can be truthfully said, I believe, that from the early days the Orthodox considered their membership of WCC in terms of spiritual and a formal physical presence, as a like-minded group, rather than as a commitment to the issues of social justice and participation of women. From Geneva, the questions asked were "Are the gifts and willingness of women being used to the best advantage by the Church?" and "Are women, married or not, being helped by the Church to understand the problems of the age as they affect women, to play their part in modern life as Christians and as women?" These questions are still relevant for us today.

Women committed to the early ecumenical movement had also been activists for women's suffrage, marital equality and the right to education. They challenged the Church and its discriminatory attitudes and practices towards women in the same way that they challenged the state. They perceived themselves as both world citizens and faithful members of the Church. The structure of their society mirrored the churches, where women served in roles subordinate to the patriarchy, whether in the person of hierarch, priest, father or husband. Church law supported the state, and cultural traditions were granted religious authenticity by the state.

Delegates may be surprised to learn that the issue of the ordination of women, whether as deacons or priests, was mentioned in all the Orthodox responses in 1947, as were issues concerning women's biology and the lack of opportunity to serve the Church. Of most interest was the detailed and open report from the Russian Orthodox community in Paris. This thorough report reflected the activities and interest of women in the community, most often émigrés from Russia and also those women who had over time married into the community and joined the Church. The influence of the Russian Student Christian Movement established in 1923 in Paris cannot be overrated. Some Orthodox women were arrested and deported during the second world war for their activities with the resistance and for hiding Jewish children who had been provided with false certificates of baptism by Fr Lev Gillet. Other women continued their work for homeless and destitute people, especially Russian émigrés, in Marseilles, Lyon and Paris. Included in the list of great defenders at the Holocaust Museum in Washington DC was the name of Mother Maria Skobstova, eventually canonized for her work in May 2004. Mother Maria asserted,

> We must not allow Christ to be overshadowed by regulations, customs, traditions, aesthetic consideration or even piety. Ultimately Christ gave us two commandments: love God and love His people[3].

From 1949, women continued their theological studies at the newly established Women's Orthodox Theological Seminary in Paris. Over fifty women enrolled for evening classes, which encompassed biblical studies, church history, Christian ethics, philosophy, psychology and education. Correspondence courses were offered to Orthodox women in Morocco, Lebanon, Syria, Belgium and the USA. From the beginning, ecumenism was a very important component, and the doors of the academy were also open and inclusive to women in other churches, especially the Catholic Church. An important and telling influence, to be repeated for countless other Orthodox programmes

---

3. Sergei Hackel, *Pearl of Great Price. The Life of Mother Maria Skobtsova 1891-1945*, Darton, Longman and Todd, London, 1981, p. 73.

over the next fifty years, were the considerable funds provided by the WCC, through Protestant Church members, to enable the academy to function properly and enable women to receive an Orthodox theological education. The ecumenical influence on these young women resulted in some taking further studies in England at Selley Oaks, a well-respected college for training missionaries and the positive practice of ecumenism, and continuing on to Oxford University for graduate studies. Militza Zernof, for example, was a former RSCM member who, with her husband Nicholas Zernov, became a mentor, patron and steadfast supporter for East-West Christian dialogue through the ecumenical Fellowship of St Alban and St Sergius, now based in Oxford, England. There is still a history to be written about these women and the role of the Academy in Paris, especially its emphasis on international and ecumenical relationships.

An informative and illuminating surprise response came from the Church of Greece. The report was authored by Thalia Woyla, a Greek Orthodox woman active in the National Organization of Christian Solidarity and the International Red Cross. She made mention of the Christian Women of Volos, a society started by Bishop Joachim Alexopoulos in 1936 for social work and education and support for the International Red Cross during the occupation. The efforts of volunteer women during the war and the founding of the Eusebia Sisterhood emphasized that women were fulfilling valuable roles in society that the church endorsed and encouraged. Although these roles were encouraged, one Coptic Orthodox woman was discerning enough to comment in her report that, while freedom for piety, charity and philanthropy for women was one thing, in the church "she must always remember the bounds in which she may work". Such was the standard of education and intellectual ability of many women in Cairo and Alexandria that they were employed by the government in social services for various departments; but their same skills were ignored or dismissed by their churches. The Cairo report also noted that charity work of Coptic Orthodox women was most often by those wealthy enough to have servants at home, a parallel to the 19th-century philanthropic and social justice advocates for women in England and America.

It is vital to bear in mind the reflective and cautionary words of Kathleen Bliss, secretary of the commission and the author of the final report and publication, The Service and Status of Women in the Churches. She wrote in 1954,

> A danger lies in the very virtues of women, their ability to make sacrifices and raise money and the nature of their organized work. Few of them think theologically and few theologians turn their minds to the enormous work done by women and ask what it means in term of the doctrine of the Church... for too many women the only work they can do for, and be approved by, the Church is work for and with women – the Church within the Church[4].

Indeed, in an earlier century, another woman wrote, "Men think that self-sacrifice and servitude is the most charming of all the cardinal virtues for women... and in order to keep it in healthy working order they make opportunities for its illustration as often as possible". The question for this consultation is to ask how often and how truly do these statements still apply, have conditions changed and to what purpose, and, if not, why not?[5] The response from the Church of Greece to the original questionnaire was well received, not only due to the information it contained but because it stands as one of the few positive responses received from this member church. Some fifty years later, the Church of Greece was one of the few member churches that did not receive a team visit for the "Living Letters" as part of WCC's Ecumenical Decade of Churches in Solidarity with Women (EDCSW).

From the beginning of WCC, the number of Orthodox women ac-

4. Kathleen Bliss, *The Service and Status of Women in the Churches*, SCM, London, 1952, p. 6.
5. Elizabeth Cady Stanton, *The Women's Bible*, 1898.

tive within it has been miniscule, though in every decade efforts have been made to increase women's role and encourage their active participation. In the 1980s, a former ecumenist Presbyterian woman, Cynthia Wedel, reflected on the absence of Orthodox women, noting that initially there had been "dynamic, intellectual and deeply committed Orthodox women from different countries and diverse cultures"[6].

At this stage I remind you of a unique Orthodox pioneer in the women's ecumenical movement. Sarah Chakko was a member of the Malankara Syrian Orthodox Church and a leader in the student Christian movement in Madras, India; she held a master's degree in Education from University of Chicago, and was principal of an American Methodist college in Lucknow, Northern India. In 1947, she was a vice-president of the World YWCA and served on the board of Christian Higher Education and the National Council of Churches of India. Sarah Chakko travelled widely, visiting many countries and discussing issues with churchwomen of all member churches. She expressed her impatience that women with intellect and ability were taking their gifts outside the churches, into societies that appreciated them. In response to the questions on the ordination of women, she replied that the question was only part of the whole problem, that there were too many matters to discuss, "...nevertheless it surely would not be so dangerous to discuss the ordination of women". Sarah Chakko was appointed chairman to the WCC commission on the Life and Work of Women in the Church in 1949, and was nominated as a vice-president of the WCC, but died prematurely before taking up the position[7].

6. Susannah Herzel, *A Voice for Women, The Women's Department of the WCC*, WCC Publications, Geneva, p. 24.
7. M. Kurian, *Sarah Chakko: A Voice of Women in the Ecumenical Movement*, Christhava Sahithya Samithy, Kerala, 1998. One of the tasks of the WCC Ecumenical Theological Education fund is to advocate for women in theological education. One of the means of doing this is the Sarah Chakko Theological Endowment Fund. The target for the fund is to reach three million dollars in five years.

AGAPIA (1976) AND ORTHODOX CONSULTATIONS

From the 1954 report I leap forward to the well-known Agapia consultation, held in 1976 at the urging of Protestant women in the ecumenical movement. Brigalia Bam, director of the Women's Unit, together with staff Bertrice Wood and Tomoko Evdokimoff were the enthusiastic proponents at WCC who believed Orthodox women had something profound to say and offer the church. Not for the first time, the considerable budget was provided by WCC to assist the Romanian Orthodox Church in their internal hospitality; and Protestant women's groups, especially from Germany, provided funds for international travel and all administration. Most of the delegates were already involved in national and ecumenical bodies such as the YWCA, the International Red Cross, and the Middle East Council of Churches, as well as in education, academia and monasticism.

Many contemporary Orthodox women should be thankful that after much discussion it was decided that Elisabeth Behr-Sigel would be invited to be the keynote speaker. Elisabeth was professor of philosophy at the Graduate Institute of Ecumenical Studies in Paris, co-editor of Contacts, a French review of Orthodoxy, and lay president of the French Orthodox community of the Holy Trinity. To my mind, her address in Agapia remains the precursor call to Orthodox women: she challenged the view that women were not frustrated or oppressed by their place being assigned by nature and Tradition, citing that it was usually men who proffered this opinion without recourse to women. Given an opportunity to read her original draft, I noted that her phrase "that ordination was no problem for Orthodox women at present [*actuellement*]" was withdrawn from the final communiqué in favour of an unqualified disclaimer that ordination was not a question for Orthodox women at all.

Elisabeth also referred to the need to re-examine the rituals and prayers in relation to the uncleanness of women –including forty days after childbirth and the prayers following a miscarriage– and especially the theological implications of exclusion from sacramental practices. She urged the involvement of women in the critical issues of contraception and abortion and all matters of reproductive health: prior to this, men alone discussed their own views and theological interpretations and pronounced for all. Agapia opened the dialogue for Orthodox women across their jurisdictions, outside their comfort zones, and women of considerable intellectual and spiritual capacity were revealed to each other and to the Church. While Elisabeth's address has been widely read, a Romanian Orthodox theologian, Anca-Luca Manolache, also prepared a paper in which she appealed to the men in the church,

> To adopt a mature reflection with a view to finding the right way to the recovery of half of the human race... In order for men to grow up, then mothers should stop doing so much for them, and find themselves, rather than only indulging as a controlling identity of motherhood[8].

Agapia emerged with six recommendations relating to anticipated issues of family, monasticism, society, education, church services, witness and ecumenism. These wide recommendations no doubt will again appear at this consultation but, I hope, with an advanced perspective on our actions, global and local networking, and both professional and lay scholarship, encouraging better outcomes now thirty years after Agapia.

During the fifteen years following the Agapia consultation, many women in the churches also experienced the benefits of the United Nations Decade for Women (1975-1985); the deliberations of the WCC assemblies in Nairobi (1975); and the ecumenical Sheffield consultation, *Community of Women and Men in the Church* (1981). Over this time, the contributions of Nina Sergeyevna Bobrova and Yelena Speranskyia from the Russian Orthodox Church were heard at ecumenical consultations insisting that the life of the church continue in the USSR,

---

8. Anca-Lucia Manolache, "Reflections of Human Nature and the Unity of the World", Unpublished paper presented at the Agapia consultation, September 1976, WCC Archives.

and indeed the contributions of women continued to be crucial. Before the Sheffield consultation, material was collected from local study groups, regional meetings and specific consultations held in Europe in response to a working document from WCC to find how church communities were involved ecumenically, if at all. The WCC received over 150 reports from Orthodox churches in France, the Middle East and North America. Orthodox responses were fairly predictable in their conservative views; however, the Orthodox Church in America (OCA) did promote its own guide to the study book, which was well-discussed across the dioceses, but this contained the OCA's own questions and forgone conclusions.

At the Vancouver assembly (1983), the women's programmes (now under Director Barbel von Wattenburg Potter, later a bishop in the North Elbian Evangelical Lutheran Church, Germany) were emerging as major considerations for the work and purpose of member churches. Orthodox nuns from Romania and Russia mingled with other "women at the well" and were spoken of years later as being an illuminating spiritual presence for many women delegates. The Rhodes consultation held in 1988, though known to only a few women, was very briefly referred to at Crete. Elisabeth Behr-Sigel, a delegate but not a speaker at Rhodes, noted in her keynote address in Crete,

> [At Rhodes] both in the daring and in their intransigence, the conclusions were symptomatic of the internal tensions within the orthodox theological community in regard to the vexed question of women's ordination. The tensions found expression in Rhodes, but they were passed over in silence in the official report, which is meant to express unanimity[9].

As I cautioned before, let us be aware of consensus and unanimous

---

9. Elisabeth Behr-Sigel, "The Ordination of Women: An Ecumenical Problem", in *Crete Consultation Report*, WCC Publications, Geneva, 1990, p. 2; also in *Sobornost* 13. 1 (1991).

statements or recommendations that merely reiterate the status quo and the expected outcome and do not provide us with the tools to advance necessary change.

CONTEMPORARY INFLUENCES AND OUR RESPONSE

The most influential catalyst of the last twenty years was the launch of the EDCSW (1988-98) under Director Anna Karin Hammar (Church of Sweden). She was succeeded by Aruna Gnanadason (Church of South India) in 1991, who was an enthusiastic and challenging supporter of Orthodox women, together with Teny Pirri-Simonian (Armenian Apostolic Church) at WCC and the Rev. Beate Stierle (Lutheran Church of Germany), director at the Ecumenical Institute at Bossey near Geneva. Accompanying all the official dialogue were the underlying programmes for reform being undertaken in sister churches. Feminist historians and theologians developed a paradigm for historical and academic research and scholarship based on a "hermeneutics of suspicion" for reading biblical texts with new eyes, finding the women of scripture and researching women's history with new methods of critical analysis.

Secular society was changing in such rapid fashion that Orthodox women were also caught in the bind of two separate spheres – their professional positions and intellectual value in the secular workforce and their expected traditional role as nurturer and servant in their church lives. In the latter, very few women could hope to be employed even if they were graduates from an Orthodox seminary. The rules and regulations expected by their church communities were becoming less important among the mainstream issues for women and men, in both the West or East, of equal opportunities for employment; sexual harassment and assault; contraception and abortion; medical research in reproductive technology; domestic violence and double standards in moral expectations; child sexual assault and pornography; homosexuality and the place of gay and lesbians Christians in churches and society; and the HIV-Aids pandemic.

It was not until 1990 that the second consultation was held in Crete. This came after the steering committee met in Cairo in 1989 to determine the agenda at the instigation and expense of the women's desk at WCC. The theme "Church and Culture" was a concerted endeavour to move forward, acknowledging the work already achieved by individual women. The steering committee in Cairo represented both Eastern and Oriental families of the Orthodox Church, bringing traditional and modern attitudes to the planning of the Crete meeting and to the EDCSW. The interesting aspect in Cairo was that the women were not hampered by the presence of any male colleagues, clergy or laity—an unusual occurrence. Sometimes one questions whether we are indeed trusted to debate without the input or supervision of men, especially when their presence is a surprise. It was in Cairo that we met with Connie Tarasar, who had been at Agapia and was well-known in ecumenical circles and especially church education in the OCA. Connie was remembered for her critical observations of the men speakers at Agapia, whom she believed had been sent to speak specifically for the glorification of motherhood and against ordination even though the women had not intended it for the agenda. They, in fact, opened the discussion on ordination and the door cannot be closed.

We also met with Marie Bassili Assaad, a Coptic Orthodox woman and sociologist, who held a senior position at the WCC as deputy general secretary and chair of the commission on Women in Church and Society and continues her work with the poorest of the poor in Cairo, those who make their existence out of other peoples' rubbish. Marie also contributed her scholarly research on female genital mutilation as practised in Egypt and Ethiopia by both Moslem and Christian families. She was an important catalyst and contributor to the WCC study of the impact of religious teachings on women published in 1990. Recognized as having a very strong voice for justice and social equality for women, she also served on the Council of Women called by His Holiness Pope Shanouda III, who was gracious in receiving the steering committee group at a public meeting and later in a private audience.

The three issues chosen for discussion in Crete were based on the theme of Church and culture, with specific study groups centered on issues of ministry; human sexuality and double standards; and the place and participation of women in the Church. As a delegate, I could clearly see that concerns about the complexities of human sexuality left the most questions to be explored. We know that all aspects of questions of sexuality create social, ethical, theological and personal dilemmas for women. The influence of culture and tradition, and indeed whether the women were from the diaspora or homeland, directed the detail of the discussions. What emerged overall was the measure of prohibitions against women on account of their gender and fecundity. There is no more contentious moral or ethical issue for women in society and the churches today than open discussion on family planning, contraception and abortion. Notwithstanding the strong and intransigent theological view of the church, many faithful Orthodox women question the rules regarding church control of their bodies and consider family planning and termination of a pregnancy as a private matter between husband and wife. For many Orthodox women, the militant voices of "right to life" too often sound hypocritical in the mouth of the church, which through much of its history has managed to co-exist with war, genocide and capital punishment. Women urged the church to open this dialogue with women, and understand the difficulties of their lives and why such decisions are made.

The dialogue on ministry in Crete was the same as usual –albeit there was more of it– as continues to be the case whenever the topic is discussed. The diaconate was seriously debated here and yet again in Istanbul in 1997. Important questions laid the foundation of disussion: "What does the ministry really mean and what form it should take in the 21st century?" and "Why can't both married men and women serve as deacons?" It was emphasized that the role of male deacons be re-assessed to reflect its social responsibility, not only its liturgical function. Elisabeth Behr-Sigel cautioned women not to wish for yet another role that was in servitude rather than service. In many ways we are not entirely sure what we mean by our ministry; for nearly all of us, we do not consider the ordination debate to be the be-all and end-all of ministry.

However, we do expect the Church to take our questioning seriously, to involve us in the debate. By this, I don't just mean an esoteric dialogue by learned theologians, men or women, already committed to one point of theology and not willing to listen to other arguments. I mean an involvement of laity as well. Even those of us without theological education – we are also the Church. We should remind ourselves constantly of the words of Sergius Bulgakov, speaking in 1927 at the First World Conference on Faith and Order in Lausanne, that "the laity no less than the clergy has its place and value in the Church as a whole. Our status is... a special order, imparted by the confirmation of holy oil... no part of the Church can claim infallibility over or against the other for even bishops and patriarchs in church history have shown they can fall into error!"[10]

It is our responsibility as laywomen to call to account our exclusion in so many areas of decision making and participation in the life of the Church because of our gender. This prejudice of misogyny continues to rob the church of one half of the intellect, the faithfulness, the knowledge, the commitment to the fullness of the faith. Of course, many here can attest to their place in church life. Our presence here is testament to that. But can we truthfully say we are fully engaged, appreciated and involved in church life in the same way that we often are in our secular professional, community or indeed family lives. When we speak of younger people these days, we immediately start the debate on the third discussion theme from Crete –and that is all aspects of human sexuality. This is not a comfortable area of discussion for any church– or indeed for other religious faiths. Society has moved so quickly that we have found ourselves floundering and failing to respond. In the face of our

10. Sergius Bulgakov, *The Orthodox Church* [1935], trans. revised Lydia Kesich, SVS Press, Crestwood, 1988, p. 259.

inadequacy, it has been easier to retreat and make human sexuality a forbidden subject. But that cannot continue.

Following the Crete consultation, more changes were made in the 1990s which I will briefly refer to. First of all, funding was made available from WCC/EDCSW fund for a modest journal, *MaryMartha*, to be published for Orthodox women. This journal was published in Perth from 1991 to 1998, after which time the funding ceased. The important function of *MaryMartha* was to disseminate information about what Orthodox women were doing, writing and achieving. Reports included the original outcomes from Agapia and Crete, and especially the seminars held at the Ecumenical Institute at Bossey near Geneva. These seminars, based on feminine images and spirituality, were to promote dialogue between Orthodox and Protestant women[11] and facilitate plans for the Damascus and Istanbul consultations. The fall of the Berlin Wall in 1989 –the final symbolic collapse of the Soviet Union– had increased the diversity of women attending seminars. Orthodox women from Romania, Czech Republic and Poland were able to attend alongside their Protestant sisters from the same countries – meeting for the first time. The themes of all the seminars shared a common purpose: to explore feminine images; feminism and spirituality in the traditions; and the role of authority and women. The seminars raised awareness of diversity and challenged stereotypes.

Again at the Bossey seminars, Elisabeth Behr-Sigel, as she had in Agapia and Crete, offered her theological wisdom and experience. She asserted that while it was important to understand the feminine models of the Theotokos and the female saints, this was not always sufficient to placate the questions of women of today. She urged women to wake from their dogmatic sleep and be prepared to undertake "experiential theology". She defended the right of feminist theologians to use feminine images when speaking of God, noting that such images also exist

---

11. *The Ecumenical Review* 60.1-2 (January/April 2008).

in Orthodoxy but had not been sufficiently developed. It is true to say that the polarization of delegates did lead at times to certain tensions. Not so much a clear division of Orthodox/Protestant but rather a feminist/conservative divides. Some Orthodox were antagonistic to the term "feminist", as they were unfamiliar with wide range of feminist theology and the work of Catholic and Protestant feminist theologians. It is pleasing that as a result of a course directed by Prof. Petros Vassiliadis on feminist hermeneutics at the Aristotle University in Thessaloniki, Orthodox women are now undertaking feminist theology studies. The times are changing, even though at a snail's pace for many, but in enlightening and illuminating ways for many others.

During the same period of the 1990s, Orthodox women were also engaged in dialogue through organizations such as the Ecumenical Forum of European Christian Women, the European Women's Synod, World Day of Prayer and the European Society of Women in Theological Research. The Women's Orthodox Ministry Education Network (WOMEN) and the publication of the *St Nina Quarterly* in the USA also received seed grants through the EDCSW funds. Sometimes we are fortunate to find other journals –together with reports of organizations, seminars and conferences– that enrich and inform us and extend our knowledge of each other and how we exercise our particular ministry in the churches.

However we know our greatest impediments to a sustainable global Orthodox women's network is twofold. First is our sense that without the permission and imprimatur of the bishops it can't happen because the church will not only not financially support us, but will often actively speak against us. Second, the imperialism of the English language leads to the situation whereby our own laziness prevents our access to so much excellent work in other languages. It appears to me that women in the European Union especially seem to have opportunities for far more ecumenical dialogue with women in other communions. I wonder whether the intransigence of bishops and clergy in so many diaspora jurisdictions is more to do with the fear of diluting the culture and traditions of their parishes and the need to maintain a control over their jurisdictional boundaries.

Between 1993 and 1996, the EDCSW promoted a unique programme to the member churches. They planned visits to all the churches with a team referred to as "Living Letters", reflecting the letter of Christ "written not in ink but the Spirit of the Living God, not on tablets of stone but on tablets of human hearts"[12]. Four themes were adopted by the EDCSW: violence against women (an issue still only narrowly discussed in Orthodox communions); women's participation in church life; global economic injustice and its effect on women; and racism against women. As a reader of the final report to be sent to the WCC assembly in 1998, I can attest to many alarming stories told by women in the churches. Final reports were written, compiled, edited and sent to member churches for comment on the critical observations made. Attitudes and practices of discrimination and violence –physical, sexual, psychological and spiritual– against women through cultural, traditional and particular biblical understanding were glaringly obvious, and it was difficult to restrain criticism in many reports. The report on meeting with the Orthodox churches in North America noted that "current social and legal pressures on clergy misconduct and homosexuality will force them onto some agendas in the churches, but issues of women's full participation, domestic violence or women's choices on abortion etc don't seem to demand any focus". There was an undercurrent of denial that many of the social and moral issues in secular society had any place in the discussion of the churches.

The Orthodox Church in America received praise from the team who remarked "we were positively surprised about the inclusiveness of the OCA as this is not common knowledge in the ecumenical movement". In his response to the presentation of the final EDCSW report at

12. Leonie B. Liveris, *Ancient Taboos and Gender Prejudice: Challenges for Orthodox Women and the Church*, Ashgate Publishing, Aldershot, UK, 2005, p. 186ff.

the Harare assembly in 1998, Metropolitan Ambrosius of Finland stated that many churches were reluctant to receive and work with the decade project as it was perceived as a feminist movement – though he added, on reflection, we might need that too. He expressed his shock at the amount of violence and economic injustice women suffered whether culturally conditioned or not. Too often it was revealed that a theology of suffering of the cross, wherein many churchwomen accepted and experienced violence and discrimination in silence, was accepted not only in secular society but also in their families and church communities[13].

CHALLENGES FOR THE FUTURE

On 22 May 2008 –"Corpus Christi", an important feast day for the West– the Rev. Kay Maree Goldsworthy was consecrated bishop in the church of God, St George's Anglican Cathedral, in Perth, Western Australia, my home city. For some within the Anglican communion and sister churches, this was a sign of moving away from the Church, a sign of disobedience to the scriptures, a sign of Western feminism finding its ultimate goal in the bestowing of Episcopal authority on a woman. This is the reasoning that finds the Orthodox Church welcoming disaffected Anglican priests who cannot abide the thought of authority from a woman, who in their theology cannot be "in persona Christi". And yet many others rejoiced in this consecration, they applauded, they called "*axios*", and they thanked God for the benefits of her blessed ministry to her diocese that will be enhanced by her spiritual, intellectual, pastoral and administrative capacity. Many Orthodox women who have been committed to the ecumenical movement for decades and who have listened to the voices of Anglican, Catholic and Protestant women will understand how this ordination has come at this time and will rejoice for Bishop Kay Goldsworthy and her community. But will we?

13. *Living Letters, A Report of Visits to the Churches during the EDCSW*, WCC Publications, Geneva, 1998.

Shall we continue to join the voices of condemnation without examining properly and with heartfelt prayer how our own church defines ministry and the ordination of women, whether as deacons or as priests? Or shall we dare to ask the question "Why not?" To dismiss this question is to deny that it has indeed been mentioned by Orthodox women in ecumenical meetings since 1947. Some years after the first meeting in Agapia, Orthodox women met again in Istanbul. The carefully phrased words in the recommendations do not truly reflect the desire for some delegates to engage in scholarship to seek out the "why not" to the question of ordination to the diaconate and the priesthood. A question, though answered, was pre-empted and inconclusive in Rhodes. The question was more openly addressed by theologians at a meeting the previous year between Orthodox and Old Catholic theologians, where the conclusion was that "there is no theological reason why women should be ordained, and, there is no theological reason why women should/could be ordained".

Surely such ambiguity requires of us to explore further with the most rigorous research and theology, to not only engage in dialogue but allow it to filter down into the dioceses and parishes for lay women and men to also engage in the question. My analysis is that the reluctance to engage reflects a misogynist fear of matriarchy – a fear that somehow women might preach the word of God and, as Elisabeth Behr-Sigel wrote, "her hands might also hold the blessed body and blood of Christ" to the people. Many years ago a Catholic woman, Frances Croake Frank, wrote the following verses:

Did the woman say,
When she held him for the first time in the
Dark dank of a stable.
After the pain and the bleeding and the crying.
"This is my body; this is my blood'?

Did the woman say
When she held him for the last time in the dark

rain on a hilltop
After the pain and the bleeding and the dying
"This is my body; this is my blood'?

Well she said it to Him then
For dry old men
Brocaded robes belying barrenness
Ordain that she say it not for him now[14].

It is not a new question, nor is it necessarily a result of the second wave of feminism of the 1970s or of the feminist influences of the West. It is a question that has arisen from the realization that the service of women in the Church is more than the servitude of women in the church, and a recognition of the lack of opportunity in our structures and tradition to bring forth our promising ministries into the whole experience of life and the church.

However, there are many more issues besides sacramental ministry. The six recommendations from Agapia in 1976 remain as important and unresolved today. Do we still respond to the description of our inaction by Elisabeth Behr-Sigel that

> women feel at ease in the warm liturgical atmosphere of the parish; they are in a comfortable cocoon and ask no question as if the social life outside had no connection with the rituals of the liturgy. It is out of laziness rather than Christian humility on their part that women do not bother to ask themselves where their responsibility does not require them to play a more active part in the spiritual guidance of the community[15].

14. Frances Croake Frank, "Did the Woman Say?", *National Catholic Reporter*, 21 December 1979.
15. Elisabeth Behr-Sigel, "The Meaning of the Participation of Women in the Life of the Church", in Constance Tarasar and Irina Kirillova (eds.), *Orthodox Women: Their Role and Participation in the Orthodox Church*, WCC Publications, Geneva, 1977, p 17-19.

The Crete recommendations in 1990 called for further study and discussion on human sexuality, even the more contentious issues. These are still more important today as we face the multitude of complexities arising from basic ethical questions about life itself, through to such phenomenon as the trafficking of women and children for the purpose of their sexual degradation and slavery, which cannot continue without a serious preventive input from the Orthodox churches. Too many of our women are being enslaved in this manner from Orthodox countries, and we need to encourage the church to be more vocal and active in stemming this godless tide of human misery. We need to raise far more awareness of this human tragedy through education within the churches and take responsibility for the lives of these young women and children. Although there is a steady small but growing number of Orthodox women receiving theological education or using their other professional qualifications for church work, perhaps we should ask how relevant much of this education is when it comes to the raw, real issues of life today.

Can we claim a growing influential presence within the church, except in our roles as mothers and educators of children and youth. We who are here have perhaps been fortunate to find a community parish, priest or bishop sympathetic to the hopes we have for our future roles in the church. Leadership that has supported the emergence of women as parish council presidents, choir directors, youth leaders, administrators, academy lecturers and child educators. But we cannot be complacent, we are in fact not the "norm" – we are too often viewed, both by laity and clergy, as the "other". We must understand that acceptance at a particular time may in fact be revoked with a change in the order of things. Not all clergy or bishops care for an enhanced role of women beyond motherhood, youth education and social service.

There have been five international consultations involving Orthodox women. Four held in partnership with the WCC –Agapia (1976), Crete (1990), Damascus (1996) and Istanbul (1997)– and the fifth held in Rhodes (1988) under the auspices of Patriarch Dimetrios 1. A few women here today were present at some of these meetings, and indeed were speakers. Resolutions and reports followed the consultations, and many here will have accessed at least the recommendations through websites and publications. However, despite the enthusiasm and obvious commitment by the delegates, one cannot claim in any way that the recommendations were more than an affirmation of existing roles and ministries for women, with only a tentative and conservative suggestion for the re-emergence of the role of deaconess. Contrary to critical articles written by those not at the meetings and with reference only to the recommendations, some discussions, albeit tentative and by only a few, took place on the ordination of women to the priesthood. These discussions and recommendations were resolved by consensus, and in the final reports were not presented as challenges to offend the sensibilities or sensitivities of bishops or clergy, or indeed women back home in the parishes.

Finally, while the Damascus and Istanbul consultations again revisited the recommendations of 1976 and 1990 –including education, ministry and sexuality– we still move very slowly on some recommendations, or not at all on most. Now in June 2008, we reach Volos where once again we have a unique opportunity provided by the WCC and the Academy to accept a responsibility to engage in a deep self-criticism. We can to raise these concerns and challenges that I have briefly shared with you from the past sixty years of our churches ecumenical relationships. We can move to positive, practical and meaningful initiatives appropriate for the 21st century.

Throughout my address I endeavoured to share the stories and achievements and, yes, even advancement of some very few women in our Orthodox churches. But in light of how women in our sister churches have challenged and witnessed their faith, I fear I must mark us as timid, as remaining under the authority of patriarchal structures, whether clergy or laity. We continue to allow the iron bands of history and culture to hold our minds, and therefore our bodies, frozen in space. We have no real movement of women – we only have strong women here and there doing extraordinary things: women in academe raising questions of theology and history; women in social justice programmes working against the international trafficking of poor and vulnerable young women; women in parish and community outreach programmes to the poor and homeless; women teaching in mission schools. We have some few writers, but alas very few with courage to speak their minds and very few willing to speak of themselves as "feminist", at least not in church circles. Publishing in Orthodox journals or books or even parish newsletters is often edited and censored by those who do not agree with what women write, or even with women's voices being heard. Women are often treated with disrespect or worse, their prophetic words ignored with astonishing regularity.

However, I remind us all that we are many women here, as many women have also gathered over the millennia. The women who gathered around Christ were honoured. Jesus chose women as disciples and apostles, he taught women as he taught men; he performed miracles for women; he praised their faith and accepted their love. He rejected the reduction of women's worth to their reproductive functions. He defended women against arbitrary divorce by calling man to the same marital fidelity. He refused to collaborate in enforcing sexual double standard by defending the woman taken in adultery.

Most astonishing of all, we are reminded in a dismissal hymn of the resurrection that,

> the women disciples of the Lord learned from the angel the glad tidings of the Resurrection. Casting aside the ancestral condemnation, they said proudly to the Apostles: Death is overthrown and Christ our God is risen, granting His Great Mercy to the world (Dismissal hymn tone 4).

Without the audacity, faithfulness and bravery of these women, who indeed would have said the words "Christ is risen"? Surely we cannot feel other than empowered to bring our biblical history, our ecumenical history, our past witness, our desire for future work and our prophetic words to the Church and be validated, honoured and invited to be equal participants in all we have been called to do through our common baptism in Christ.

CURRENT THEOLOGICAL ISSUES AND CHALLENGES ON WOMEN'S PARTICIPATION IN THE CHURCH

DIMITRA KOUKOURA

Twenty years after the historic conference of Rhodes in November 1988, the issues concerning the full participation of women in the life of the Church have been emphasized and in some way discussed by a limited number of Orthodox Christians. What is of greater interest for our meeting is the degree to which the faithful (πληρώματα) of the Orthodox churches have been informed about these issues.

We believe that an efficient and extensive update can accelerate the implementation of the conclusions that have been accepted by all Orthodox churches. Such a decision will enrich the life of the Church with the creative presence of women and will ensure the co-existence of "correct faith" (*Orthodoxia*) and "correct action" (*Orthopraxia*) in the modern world.

Orthodox Christians began dealing with women's issues after receiving pressure from other Christian families in the World Council of Churches (WCC). Since the beginning of the 20th century, when the general feminist movement brought significant changes in the social presence of women, churches in Europe and the USA expanded the roles of women in the lives of Christian communities, culminating in the ordination of women. The ordination of women was certainly not accepted unanimously by Protestant churches nor by the Anglican church, which led to further fragmentation[1]. Roman Catholics reacted by rejecting the idea of ordination[2], but at the same time they increased the participation of women in holy worship, as well as in the teaching and guiding work of the Church.

---

1. These were Protestant groups mainly in the U.S.A., which vigorously resisted this innovation and were later labeled fundamentalists.
2. Cf. the encyclical *Lumen Gentiumm*, 4, 197, where the people are encouraged to participate in the church's work of salvation according to their gifts and potential.

Orthodox Christians were astonished by this new reality; nevertheless, they had to face it, as they are official members of the WCC according to inter-Orthodox synods. The issue of female ordination was prominent in all theological discussions of the last three decades of the 20th century in the WCC, so the Orthodox response had to be well supported.

In 1974, the issue "The Society of Men and Women within the Church" was the object of study in the department of Faith and Order of the WCC, apparently influenced by a similar program of the UN concerning the full participation of men and women in the life of human society. In the same year, about thirty representatives of Orthodox churches convened for the first time at the Orthodox Centre of Chambésy with the sole purpose of providing the first concrete Orthodox responses to a variety of questions, which may be summarized as follows:

- To what degree do women participate in the life of your church?
- Why is it that Orthodox delegations representing the entirety of the Christian body in inter-Christian dialogues do not include women?
- Why is the ordination of women rejected?

In the year 1975, with the initiative and funding of the WCC programme on Education and Renewal, Orthodox women convened in the Romanian monastery Agapia and had their first opportunity to discuss the burning issues that were already concerning the Protestant world. The participants in this inter-Christian dialogue looked forward to the findings of this conference with great expectation. This interest was fuelled by the fact that, until that time, Orthodox men (mostly high-ranking clerics and to a lesser degree lay academic teachers) always represented the bodies of Orthodox churches, and responded to a variety of issues, representing men and women, the clergy and the laity. This choice obviously reflected the structures of patriarchal societies, where "the man has an opinion on public issues, while the woman deals with domestic affairs".

In the year 1981, the questionnaires that had been sent by the WCC's Faith and Order department to all church members three years earlier were processed in Sheffield, England. These question-naires contained crucial theological questions about the nature and the position of women in the life of the Church and the possibility of their ordination. As expected, the feeble Orthodox responses promp-ted a more serious preoccupation with this issue, and the organization of a representative inter-Orthodox conference.

In Rhodes in the year 1988, the main funding came from the WCC, the summons was issued by the Ecumenical Patriarchate, and the re-sponse of the Orthodox world was satisfactory. Indeed, the number of females participating was unprecedented, reaching 33% of those attending. In previous meetings, very few Orthodox women had par-ticipated in theological dialogue, instead performing auxiliary services like translation and secretarial work. The conference in Rhodes was truly important, because Orthodox Christians officially and seriously dealt with significant issues that concerned the witness to Orthodoxy in the modern world.

Rhodes was followed by a number of interesting inter-Orthodox meetings, some of which are particularly important due to the signifi-cant participation of Orthodox women and their published proceed-ings: Crete (1990); Damascus (1996); and Constantinople (1997), within the program me of the EDCSW. On these occasions, Orthodox women had the opportunity to discuss their problems at length and to publish their findings.

Another important programme, which concerned the very essence of the WCC and focused on ecclesiology, was entitled "On Being Church", and included the issues of women with the study programme *Women's Voices and Visions on Being Church*. In the year 2001, the ba-sic core of veteran Orthodox women, empowered by new dynamic at-tendees, convened in Geneva and surveyed anew the Orthodox reality in relation to the roles of women under completely different histori-cal circumstances. Following 1989, the traditionally Orthodox coun-tries of Europe escaped the burden of communist regimes, while the new social conditions offered unprecedented possibilities to women.

Among them, it is worth mentioning women's access to theological studies and the teaching of religion in primary and secondary level education.

A noteworthy general observation, based on all these Orthodox conferences, either the mixed one in Rhodes or the exclusively feminine ones, is that they all reached the same conclusions.

Ordination is not an issue of concern for Orthodox Church bodies, and is therefore not discussed at length, although the roles of women are indeed limited in the lives of Orthodox communities and parishes. In this respect, many things should change. Therefore, for Orthodox women the approach to reality was not based, as is feminist theology, on the famous principle "through the eyes of women" and the use of inclusive language. Men and women certainly participate in the same gifts of the Holy Spirit and spiritual experience of salvation (soteriology). Furthermore, scientific accuracy leads Orthodox men and women alike to the same conclusions about the historical framework through which Christianity spread in the first centuries, whereby social conditions led to the marginalization of women.

What was most important in these particular proceedings, however, was the free expression of Orthodox women and the conclusions that were reached in common with men, in spaces where the Orthodox witness exists. The equal public presence of men and women is now taken for granted in modern civilization, replacing the social dominance of men that was based on the dictate: "Woman, you don't know anything, the man of the house is talking now"!

This habit of male dominance, when it persists in carrying the seal of holiness in the social practice of Orthodox churches, poses a more general and very significant problem for Orthodox Christians. It is not a theological, ecclesiological, ontological or soteriological problem, but an issue of interpreting Tradition. It concerns the choice between a static and a dynamic overview of a living tradition of two thousand years, and the possibility or impossibility of Orthodox Christians distinguishing the mutable and immutable elements of Tradition. Eventually we need the deepest faith in the Gospel and a sufficient knowledge of our era in order to accomplish what the great teachers of our Church –the men and women saints of God– did in the age-long duration of our ecclesiastic history. They experienced the enduring faith in the Triune God and responded to the challenges of their time. This is what we are called upon to achieve, because Tradition does not refer to the preservation of old changeable social practices, but a solid faith in Jesus Christ.

It is obvious that all the issues discussed at various conferences can be resolved through this perspective. However, delicate actions and a wide dissemination of information are needed, so that Orthodox Christians may recognize the unchanging elements our faith and the practices that originate in non-Christian beliefs. These are variable elements that have seeped into the life of the church and gradually acquired a false holiness and a permanency. Such a case is the issue of "clean and unclean women".

Informing the masses can defeat even the most vigorous resistance of small, fanatical groups in conservative circles. Any decisive effort for progress in the life of the Church usually collides with the compact front of so-called defenders of Orthodoxy, hindering activity and leading to inertia. Among the factors opposing any rejection of old habits and implementation of new ones is the mentality of some Orthodox women themselves, the ones who champion the "theology of the kitchen", which will be discussed later.

As noted above, the ordination of women has not been a central issue in any inter-Orthodox conference. It was proven unanimously that this was not an internal need of the female members of the ecclesiastic bodies, which would seek external support in order to be expressed and satisfied. However, the issue of expanding the roles of women in the life of the Church was central; the demands for changes were unanimous and unchallenged, since these roles are determined by the mutable social environment and not by the immutable truth of the gospel.

Orthodox Christians evinced a variety of reactions to the topic of female ordination: irony, indifference, but also gravity. Several people revealed insecurity as they were faced by a new challenge, venturing into irony, while others hastened to accumulate counter-arguments that lacked depth. Some responses were particularly sober and creative.

We commemorate the late Prof. Nikolaos Matsoukas, who pointed out the responsibility of theological research to respond to each era's challenges as soon as they emerge, even if they are of no immediate concern to the Church. Theology must always offer the truth of the gospel according to the needs of each age, because the same issues might arise at a later time. Even if they never arise, the duty of theology is to articulate a responsible and crystal-clear word. This position resulted in the presentation of several postgraduate research papers by Prof. Matsoukas's students as well as his own paper at a joint conference of the School of Theology at Aristotle University of Thessaloniki and the department of Faith and Order. There, he concluded with unquestionable biblical and dogmatic argumentation that the rejection of ordination is founded on the "argument from Tradition" (*argumentum e traditione*), and on the wholly negative results that would come of implementing unnecessary changes in the life of the Church. Potentially accepting the ordination of women here and now, without genuine and internal demand, would cause greater harm (in the storm of reactions) than benefit (the equal treatment of women). Furthermore, the variety of gifts of men and women and their respective uses in the life of the parishes satisfactorily answers the question of female ordination.

In a comparison of the findings of the afore-mentioned conferences, we find they all detail the possibility of fuller female participation in the didactic and guiding work of the church on all levels of ecclesiastic administration as well as worship. References are made to human sexuality, the issue of clean and unclean women, the more extensive role of nuns and priests' wives in the work of the parish, and the revival of the order of deaconess.

So far there has been agreement on how to expand the participation of women. The following are examples of areas for such participation:

- education and Christian instruction at all levels;
- spiritual guidance on marriage, baptism, family, illness etc.;
- social care for the elderly, orphaned, marginalized, abused etc.;
- work with the young;
- direction of choirs, participation as choristers and readers etc.;
- communication and publications;
- ecclesiastic administration and participation in decision making on all levels;
- delegations for inter-Christian dialogues.

The question posed here is, when will all this be implemented?

It will happen slowly, for many reasons. It usually takes time for all those concerned to realize that changes in society should parallel an upgrading of female roles in the life of the Church. It also takes time to prepare women for new roles, as we saw with regard to the ecumenical movement. In other cases, the change will come naturally. The lack of men in certain sectors will be covered automatically by women, or if a woman is unquestionably superior for a position – for example, as an academic– she will take precedence.

In issues of education, social care and guidance of youth the active role of women is and has been taken for granted since the earliest of Christian centuries. The classes of widows, virgins and deaconesses performed such services according to the needs of their time. Today, these can be coordinated through electronic networks and supported by data banks. We consider that the potential for participation these sectors is constantly increasing, since the reliability, devotion and effectiveness of women in these areas has never been doubted, while their performance is often lauded and responsibilities are gladly allocated to them by the men.

Thirty years after Agapia, the –then unattainable– gift of theological education for women is already a pleasant reality. This is clearly the result of the attainment of equal rights for women in public education, to which ecclesiastic education on all levels voluntarily complied in all countries of the world, and especially the former Marxist states. All this has been realized in relation to the education of women in schools of theology and the teaching of religion in the first two levels of education. However, the instruction of women in clerical seminaries and third-level education has not seen radical changes, since the men have temporal precedence in order to prepare for the appropriate positions.

It is a matter of little time for the ratio of women teaching theology in academic institutions to multiply. In 1993, the ratio was 1 woman to 30 men, while today nearly a third of the teachers are women: 9 women to every 29 men.

However, ecclesiastic administration on all levels remains a male dominion, while the activities of charity councils remains a significant outlet for female dynamism. This scenario preserves the old dichotomies of men and women in social practices and does not project their co-existence in society or their collective efforts in the life of the parish. In Greece, one or two cases have been seen where local bishops imposed mixed ecclesiastic councils, despite some negative male reactions. No other similar initiatives have been reported.

Mixed choirs are well-established; however, a talented woman with good knowledge of Byzantine music has almost no chance of leading a Byzantine choir, even if she is superior to a male candidate. Visualize a male-dominated choir in an Orthodox church in front of the murals of saints, men and women: the murals teach us the equal participation in the sanctifying grace of God, while the choir exhibits the persistence of male-dominated society! The former is the gift of God, while the latter is habit that may eventually be forced to change. Even now, if no male chorister is present, it is not unusual for a woman who knows this craft to fulfill his duties. However, if a man appears, she must stand aside, or even withdraw!

The official revival of deaconesses seems to be stalled for two main reasons. The first is that most of the services of deaconess are already performed by nuns or by women who offer service to the Church. The second, and the greatest, difficulty for their revival seems to be the idea of the public transmission of Holy Communion during Holy Liturgy. This would entail the entrance of the deaconess into the sanctuary and her public co-existence with priests in the area of the altar. For the moment this seems to be a difficult concept not only for men to digest, but for some women as well: those who have stereotypical views on the services of female members of the church and who rely upon everything taught to them by male spiritual teachers. Women themselves, with sufficient theological ignorance, have preserved pre-Christian traditions, customs and various obsessions.

The result is the "theology of the kitchen", which accepts, with no objection, the postpartum and menstrual uncleanliness of women. This mentality leads many women to ask on Good Friday, "Should I bow in front of the epitaph if I am menstruating?" And priests often reply, "Of course not, because you are unclean"! All this, when the Church declares with the hymns of resurrection that Jesus on the cross redeemed us from the curse of the Law with his holy blood and that life enters the grave to raise all the dead!

The example of the epitaph is characteristic of the long list of prohibitions against women during their menstruation, which culminates in their exclusion from Holy Communion, the food of eternal life and the medicine of immortality!

This is an issue that merits enlightenment, research and even denouncement in this era of spectacular progress in biology and other natural sciences with regard to the function of the human body and the decoding –as far as possible– of the mystery of life.

Equally important is the theological research that proves the Judaic origin of these beliefs, which brought about not only the social exclusion of women in the past, but an emotional grid of guilt, uncleanliness and miasma. And all this when the woman's body is functioning naturally, participating in God's plan for the multiplication of human kind and the birth of images of the inexpressible (αρρήτου) glory of the Triune God!

CURRENT THEOLOGICAL ISSUES AND CHALLENGES ON WOMEN'S MINISTRY IN THE CHURCH
Tamara Grdzelidze

Theological reflection in the Orthodox Church with respect to gender and ministry proves that women are as highly acknowledged in their witness and service as men. The challenges, however, of their being equally represented in decision making in the life of the Church are great. The problems that prevent women's voices from being heard or taken into consideration are mostly cultural and economic, but these are serious and often disguised.

The question of the ministry of women in the Church naturally merges into the question of ordination of women, although it is not limited to it. My brief exposition of the theme will take as a starting point the present situation in the Orthodox Church: currently, the Church does not practice ordination of women.

The Orthodox in general express no reservations about the special role of women in the worldly life of our Lord Jesus Christ as well as after his death and bodily resurrection. Historically, women were there in the midst of it all, witnessing, serving, participating, mourning; in other words, women's ministry at the time of the incarnation and worldly life of Christ has not been disputed. The Mother of God is the most vivid example of witness and ministry.

What is ministry in theological terms? Any expression of ministry in this context begins with faith and witnessing and leads to service and commitment. Certainly, in Christian use "ministry" is largely associated with ordained ministry, but I will refer to ministry as a more polyvalent concept that stretches from ways of expressing one's faith to dedicated service in the name of our Lord. The whole ministry in the Church, whether ordained or lay, is placed within the baptism and the Eucharist, and thus addresses the whole life in the Church.

Let me pose another related question: Can women under the current circumstances be leaders in the Orthodox Church? Again, this question requires a qualified answer, a careful insight into terminology. Our cliché-oriented mentality links leadership exclusively with governing bodies, with persons who are in charge of finalizing decisions. But is it really so? Is leadership in the Church limited to persons in charge of decision making? And even if it is, do they make up their minds in isolation?

May I state straight away that leadership in the Church is not exclusively linked with persons ex officio, and that women, to a certain degree, participate in the leadership performed by the persons ex officio. My initial argument in this context is that well-grounded thinking expressed in a convincing way penetrates the social sphere regardless of its origin. In other words, if something remarkable is expressed, it does not matter who says it, a man or a woman – it will penetrate the social sphere. In theological terms, "When the Spirit of truth comes, he will guide you into all the truth" (John 16:13).

Ministry in the Church stretches from faith and witness to leadership, and women in one way or another participate in it. Robert Runcie, then-Archbishop of Canterbury, wrote in 1983: "It is an imperative for the churches to regain a wide concept of ministry which is not narrowed by the jurisdictional inhibitions of those who cannot recognize a ministry unless it is institutionalized by the formal authorization of a bishop, a presbyter, or a congregation"[1].

I quite like the idea, heard from an Orthodox bishop, that one receives his or her first Christian formation at home from a mother (or a grandmother). This question –what is the effect of the initial formation one receives at home– goes beyond theological competence, but a priori there must be a significant effect to be discovered by psychologists. Education received at home is among the important influences one receives in a lifetime, but this is a very small influence and does not include all women.

1. *The Community of Women and Men in the Church: The Sheffield Report 1981*, Constance F. Parvey (ed.), WCC Publications, Geneva, 1983, p.21.

What is women's ministry? How can women participate in the life of the Church?

Nobody questions the importance of diaconal work, the image of Martha, or of the monastic vocation through which women achieve incredible spiritual and material fulfillment. Monastic life is a kind of liberation of a woman from the existing constraints of patriarchal society. "The obedience to a call from On High frees her from biological and social determinism"[2].

About twenty years ago Elisabeth Behr-Sigel wrote, "Women must be called out of their silence"[3]. She stressed the importance of speaking out and reflecting with fathers, brothers, husbands, sons and male friends or colleagues on the tasks of today. Certainly, this is still valid in many contexts, especially in places where the Orthodox churches exist within societies of developing economies.

One small remark about the possible effect of globalization today. It is not the subject of our inquiry, but experience proves that globalization and technological progress, in spite of all the difficulties they bring, provide more opportunities for women in terms of equality. The time has come when a women-men confrontation leading to a dialogue between the two sexes may sound invalid. There are serious issues of the disproportionate number of men active in the church or other spheres of social life compared to women, but the concept of "confrontation" between women and men is neither helpful nor entirely justified. Certainly, this does not mean that in the Orthodox church, especially in some places, women have equal footing with men in all respects. However, there is solid ground for Orthodox women today to be sure that the social development of a global economy and theological reflection on the equality of men and women would never provide any serious foundation for a belief that women are unequal to men and therefore must confront them.

2. *Echos* 7 (1995), p. 36.
3. *Echos* 7 (1995), p. 31.

CONTINUING ISSUES

Several meetings have been sponsored by the World Council of Churches (WCC) on the issue of women in the life of the Orthodox church: Agapia (1976), Rhodes (1988), Crete (1990), Damascus (1996) and Istanbul (1997). Some of the suggestions running throughout the proceedings of those meetings have been significant to this day. Among the concerns of the report from Istanbul, for example, we see a call to stimulate lay people, to inspire "our people to take an active role in the life of the Church". Such a call is still a precious priority for the Orthodox worldwide[4].

However, some recommendations from the above-mentioned meetings I find to be irrelevant today, such as creating a special forum for women in which they can experience and engage in theological research. Such an experience would be isolated and self-sufficient in nature. On the contrary, women must "speak out" in the midst of the life, in the Church, in an authentic environment and not within an artificially created security. What can be achieved in an environment for one gender may not be valid in different circumstances.

Elisabeth Behr-Siegel wrote years ago, "We live in a time of violence that often takes on atrocities or absurd forms"[5]. This is very true with regard to our time as well. Sitting in front of a television, watching live footage from a war and eating a bowl of cereal speaks of the absurdity of life when violence takes over. Maybe it was the absence of women from the scene for centuries that led to the present violence in the world. Nowadays, there are many ways for women to apply themselves to "putting right" the ugly side of our reality.

Orthodox women should neither take a radical stand against the exi-

---

4. *The Place of Woman in the Orthodox Church and the Question of the Ordination of Woman, Inter-Orthodox Symposium, Rhodos, Greece, 30 October-7 November 1988,* Gennadios Limouris (ed.), Tertios Publications, Katerini, p. 285.
5. Elizabeth Behr-Sigel & Bishop Kallistos Ware, *The Ordination of Women in the Orthodox Church,* WCC Publications, Geneva, 2000, p. 32.

sting structures in the Church leaning to the statements for liberation of women, nor find satisfaction in the traditional teachings that sometimes sound misogynistic. We live in a time of constant thinking and interpretation, which puts every human being under the great pressure of confronting a world that ceaselessly poses questions and demands our answers. Whether we like the legacy of post-modernism or not, it is here. It is a mistake to think of the Church as an escape from this reality. The Church is the reality (in fact, a bigger reality, we believe, than the news we watch on TV) and cannot be separated from the world we live in.

Women must recognize their equality with men and their own strength in making a difference. Women must "speak out", as Elisabeth Behr-Siegel says, and believe in the value of their presence in processes taking place in the Church and elsewhere.

ORTHODOX THEOLOGICAL PERSPECTIVE ON GENDER, MINISTRY AND ORDINATION OF WOMEN

Theologically, there has been good preparatory work done for the last forty years manifesting the equality of men and women in God' creation. Women are of the same order as men, created in the image of God. "Both man and women reflect to an equal degree of the glory of Christ and partake of the grace and joy of being reborn and living in Him", wrote Metropolitan Chrysostomos of Myra, then and after of Ephesus[6]. From a theological point of view, the gender issue exists within the life of the Church, but it diminishes within the eschaton.

In order to complement the issue of women's ministry in the Orthodox church, it is reasonable to observe how theological argument on the matter has been shifting. The standard Orthodox approach to ordination of women has been for decades the following: variety of services implying variety of gifts (Acts 1:17; 1 Tim. 1:12; 2 Tim. 4:5). This is summarized by Prof. Vlassios Pheidas,

---

6. *The Place of Woman*, p. 132.

There is no superiority of man over woman because of the peculiarity of their roles in the life of the Church. The priesthood of men as a type of Christ and the function of women as a type of the mission of the Holy Spirit highlight more fully not only the inner unity and synergy of the distinguished functions of the man and the woman in the mystery of the divine economy, but also the well balanced appropriation of the Paschal mystery of Christ and the mystery of Pentecost in the mystery of the Church[7].

This approach has been challenged by some Orthodox theologians, such as Elisabeth Behr-Siegel, Metropolitan Kallistos Ware and Prof. Nikos Matsoukas,

In fact, nothing in its faith, no theological reason, seems to me to prevent the Church –if it considers it of use– from ordaining, i.e. blessing, a female Christian for the exercise of a ministry which is an expression of the universal priesthood of all the faithful, while at the same time pointing to him who is its one divine source[8].

Metropolitan Kallistos raises the question of women's leadership in the Church from the point of the nature of such a role, and he seeks the answer in the Pauline spirit of the Church being unity-in-diversity.

When we speak about "distinctive" gifts of women, we have to be on our guard against making generalizations about "woman" in the abstract, which reflect cultural stereotypes rather than the actual diversity of women in history and in the modern world. Even if women do indeed possess, as a sex, distinctive spiritual gifts, it does not therefore follow that they cannot perform the same tasks as men; we are only justified in concluding that they will perform these tasks in a different way[9].

7. Ibid., p. 196.
8. Behr-Sigel & Kallistos Ware, p. 42.
9. Ibid., p. 64.

Speaking against the validity of the traditional arguments for non-ordination of women in the Orthodox church (such as Christ choosing only male apostles, or that the Mother of God did not assume a hieratic role), Prof. Matsoukas finds them dogmatically unaccurate as well as arising *ex silentio* or *ex absentia*, which is an insufficient argument. Christ's maleness, he believes, contradicts the doctrine of Chalcedon, and he quotes from the Ambigua by Maximus the Confessor,

> First he united us in himself by removing the difference between male and female, and instead of men and women, in whom above all this manner of division is beheld, he showed us as properly and truly to be simply human beings, thoroughly transfigured in accordance with him, and bearing his intact and completely unadulterated image, touched by no trace at all of corruption[10].

None of the three above-mentioned theologians speaks strictly for the ordination of women in the Orthodox Church, but their arguments lead us to believe that this is an open question for the Orthodox and that a theological reflection on the subject should be carried on.

The issue of utmost importance for the Orthodox –and women may become pioneers in this research– is to distinguish between the Tradition and non-Tradition (i.e., history, popular piety etc.). This need has been articulated by various theologians at various occasions and Metropolitan Kallistos is one of them[11].

In the 1980s, the ordination of women in the Anglican church predicted a real threat of estrangement and interruption in a dialogue between the Orthodox and Anglicans, so much so that both sides considered continuing dialogue only between the Orthodox and those

10. *One, Holy, Catholic and Apostolic: Ecumenical Reflection on the Church*, T. Grdzelidze (ed.), Faith and Order Paper No. 197, WCC Publications, Geneva, 2005, p. 221-22.
11. Behr-Sigel & Kallistos Ware, p. 65.

Anglican churches that did not accept the ordination of women[12]. However, the Cyprus report from 2006 shows a quite different solution. It extends the framework of reflection on ministry by suggesting that,

> this issue should be considered in the wider context of the ministries of women and men within laity and the diaconate. It cannot be isolated from the wider koinonia of the Church. Our consideration of the ordination of women therefore includes consideration of all the ministries exercised by women as well as men in the Church. Agreement between Orthodox and Anglicans on the ministry of women in the presbyterate and episcopate has not been achieved. But it may be possible for us to agree on the wider ministry of lay women and the ministry of women in the diaconate[13].

I personally believe that assuming different roles of ministry in the Church within the present situation –as the Orthodox church does not practice ordination of women– provides many opportunities for women's ministry and leadership. Women with proper theological background as teachers, members of parish councils, administrators in church structures, mothers, wives, sisters, friends do have influence, and their ministry is important. These are women who are fully aware of the importance of their ministry and therefore prepared –psychologically, spiritually, intellectually– for such a role.

One small remark to encourage the Orthodox women in their ministry in the Church: as the Consultation on Ministry and Ordination in the Community of Women and Men in the Church in Germany in 2003 revealed, ordination of women in many churches has not solved

12. *The Place of Woman*, p. 282-83.
13. *The Church of the Triune God: The Cyprus Agreed Statement of the International Commission for Anglican-Orthodox Theological Dialogue 2006*, Anglican Communion Office, London, UK, 2006, p. 77.

problems related to gender issues in church life. On the contrary, often it has created unexpected problems, suggesting that we require deeper analysis of the ministry of women and men in the Church.

"MANY WOMEN WERE ALSO THERE ..." BUT WHERE? CHALLENGES AND OPEN QUESTIONS ON WOMEN'S ROLE IN THE ORTHODOX CHURCH (IN THE FRAME OF THE ECUMENICAL MOVEMENT)

ELENI KASSELOURI-HATZIVASSILIADI

My theological journey into Christian sources, especially into the Bible, but also into the writings of the Fathers, is that of searching for answers to questions about life and death, hope and despair, justice, solidarity, tolerance and love. One of the fundamental and crucial questions that continues to trouble my mind and my heart is what sort of Church Jesus Christ is calling us to experience today. From my New Testament readings, and despite the strong feeling of "a democracy of heaven" in Orthodox liturgy, I believe, that we are still in many cases far away from Jesus's vision of the Church as a loving, inclusive, just and participatory community of men and women, the people of God[1].

WOMEN'S ROLE IN ORTHODOXY AND THE FRUITS OF ECUMENICAL DIALOGUE

My participation in the World Council of Church's (WCC) women's programmes –especially in "Women's Voices and Visions on Being Church", as a member of the steering committee– consultations and seminars, and my collaboration with theologians like Aruna Gnanadason, Letty Russell, Shannon Clarkson, Nancy Cardoso Pereira, Mercy Amba Oduyoye, Sook Ja Chung, Tenny Simonian and many

---

1. According to Daniel G. Groody, following Jesus and his vision of the Church creates a certain model of spirituality: "Christian spirituality is about following Jesus, living out the values of the Kingdom of God, and generating a community transformed by the love of God and others. Lived out in its personal and public dimensions, Christian spirituality is the way in which the invisible heart of God is made visible to the world" in *Globalization, Spirituality and Justice. Navigating the Path to Peace*, Orbis Books, New York, 2009, p. 241.

others enriched my way of looking at theological questions on women's participation in the Church. Although I experienced many moments of sisterhood, respect and love, I also came face-to-face with the reality that in many Western theological circles, Orthodoxy has come to signify stagnation in church life, strict dogmatic confessionalism, inflexibility and unwillingness to adapt to modern situations: that is, an "Eastern phenomenon" vis-à-vis "the Western mentality". Another observation was that although I am Orthodox in faith and dogma, I was reading my orthodox tradition a bit differently than my Orthodox sisters from other regions, mainly because of our diverse cultural and historical backgrounds. Culture and context always play a crucial role in our hermeneutical approach and we should never underestimate them.

The above opinion of Orthodoxy of other Christians is not only the result of the fact that the Orthodox reject all possibility of ordaining women to the priesthood. Of great importance is also the Orthodox understanding of Tradition and its relation to the present. The impossibility –according to the Orthodox– of isolating the problem of women's ordination from the totality of Tradition has and continues to create a number of misunderstandings, gaps and disagreements in ecumenical discussion.

As Orthodox, we are fighting with some of the following questions regarding Tradition: Is it the living memory and consciousness of the Church, the only and essential term of reference or criterion by which we discern the un-brokenness of the church's life and identity during her pilgrimage through history? Is Tradition a product, or a sequence of products, of history, in the light of which it is re-evaluated, judged or rejected?[2] How much weight are we to ascribe to the silence of Tradition? Since in the teaching of Jesus Christ and the apostles

---

2. See P. Kalaitzidis, "From the 'Return to the Fathers' to the Need for a Modern Orthodox Theology", *St. Vladimir's Quarterly* 54:1 (2010), p. 5-36, esp. 29-33.

there is no specific commandment to ordain women to the ministerial priesthood, and since for nearly two thousand years the Church has refrained from proceeding to such ordination, do we at the beginning of the 21st century have the right to take a fresh initiative in this matter?[3]

More and more Orthodox scholars support today that some of the elements of the Tradition, central and essential (especially those influenced by the historical and cultural reality) though they are, should be re-interpreted and re-evaluated[4]. I agree with Aristotle Papanikolaou, a contemporary Greek American theologian from Fordham University, that,

> Orthodoxy is, in essence, a tradition of thinking on the realism of divine-human communion manifested in the person of Jesus Christ. It is this particular core of the tradition that will shape Orthodoxy's response to central questions of a present situation, even beyond post-modernity, and that constitutes the single most important contribution that Orthodoxy can bring to ecumenical dialogue[5].

For Elizabeth Behr-Sigel, the problem, and perhaps the particular "temptation", of Orthodoxy is its inability to transfer the "vision of

3. See my article, "Der Begriff der Tradition und die Frauenordination. Ein orthodoxer Ansatz", *Ökumenische Rundschau* 2 (April 2001) p. 167-77.
4. Bishop Kallistos of Diokleia, in the new edition of *Women and the Priesthood* (Thomas Hopko (ed.), St. Vladimir's Seminary Press, New York, 1999, p. 5-54) has changed his views on the subject. He has moved in the direction of greater tentativeness about the possible ordination of women as priests and bishops in the Orthodox Church. He also demonstrates less conviction about authority of the traditional Orthodox practice on the issue and questions his own rather firm arguments against the ordination of women as bishops and presbyters drawn from the vision of the presbyter/bishop as a sacramental "icon" of Christ in the Church.
5. Aristotle Papanikolaou, "Orthodoxy, Postmodernity, and Ecumenism: The Difference that Divine-Human Communion Makes", *Journal of Ecumenical Studies* 42:4 (Fall 2007), p. 527.

an authentic community" into social reality[6]. After all, the Orthodox conception of the Church is not a communion of human beings unrelated to society and history.

A theological reflection on Tradition and women's participation (in the frame of the general issue of the participation of the laity) is nowadays indispensable[7]. The problem of their full and creative participation in the life of the Church, social and spiritual, can no longer be considered as an "external" but as an "internal" issue for Orthodox churches[8]. This "internalization"[9] should probably be understood as a reconsideration of ideas and practices, an opening up of forgotten prospects and horizons[10].

Living in a various contexts of the global community in the post-modern era, where there is an urgent need for new inspiring visions and ideas, Orthodox women are called to offer their witness according to the gospel and the richness of their liturgical and spiritual

6. See Elisabeth Behr-Sigel, *Le ministère de la femme dans l' Eglise*, Les Editions du Cerf, Paris, 1987, p. 105-15.

7. See Valerie Karras, "The Orthodox Theologies of Women and ordained ministry", in Aristotle Papanikolaou & Elizabeth H. Prodromou (eds.), *Thinking through Faith. New Perspectives from Orthodox Christian Scholars*, St. Vladimir's Seminary Press, New York, 2008, 113-58. Also Eleni Kasselouri-Hatzivassiliadi, *Feminist Hermeneutics: An Orthodox Approach* (in Greek), Thessaloniki 1998 and "Women and Orthodox Spirituality", in Annette Esser, Anne Hunt Overzee, Susan Roll (eds.), *Re-visioning Our Sources*, 1997, p. 76-85.

8. See Eva Adamtziloglou, "Is Feminist Theology Possible in the Greek Orthodox Tradition?", *Yearbook ESWTR* 4 (1996), p. 17-27.

9. "The question of the ordination of women to the priesthood … must become for us [Orthodox] a question that is asked 'from the inside'. This question requires of us all an interior freedom and a deep communion with the vision and will of God, in a prayerful silence" (Metropolitan Anthony of Sourozh, "Preface to the French Edition", in Elisabeth Behr-Sigel, *The Ministry of Women in the Church*, Oakwood Publications, Redondo Beach, CA, 1991, p. xiii-xiv, at xiv).

10. See Eleni Kaselouri-Hatzivassiliadi "Feminist Theology: A Challenge for Dialogue" (in Greek), *Orthodoxia* 2 (November 1999), p. 65-66.

tradition. Postmodernity or late modernity, as a philosophical and political movement, and the new context of this witness and mission should be viewed and understood through its three main "moments". The first moment is the postmodern "critique of modernity", which consists in unmaking modernity's contradictory impulses and results. For example, modernity promised freedom, equality and unlimited progress. What modernity produced instead was various forms of oppression, genocides, ecological disaster, and gender or other forms of discrimination. Its rampant capitalism produced extreme poverty and class inequality. The second moment is connected with the autonomous self, for postmodernity seeks the "disappearance" of the subject. The autonomous self of the Enlightenment centered meaning in itself and its belief in its unlimited power and freedom. The third moment concerns the end of universal and hegemonic definitions, discourses and world views. It calls into question the meaning of individual words, construing them as open with multiple meanings. The prevalent discourses of groups in power are overturned. Even science, seen as the site of ecological destruction, is no longer considered "objective"; it takes its place as one among many belief systems. The term "objective" itself is no longer operative. The playing field of opposing world views becomes level, even tipped toward local and alternative epistemologies[11].

These three moments have opened new perspectives for philosophical thought and theology. Rapid changes have already appeared regarding the contextuality of theology, the methods and the tools of interpretating the Bible, the "theological turn" of phenomenology, the growth of liberation theologies, feminist theologies etc. For example, by calling into question the Enlightenment project, postmodernism enables feminist theologians to interrogate the male bias of even

---

11. Susan Dolan-Henderson, "Post-modernism", in Letty M. Russel & J. Shannon Clarkson (eds.), *Dictionary of Feminist Theologies*, Westminster John Knox Press, 1996, p. 217-18.

so-called liberal theologies. All these in connection with globalization and multiculturalism (phenomena that have dramatically empowered poverty, social injustice, violence) are calling Orthodox theology and theologians for answers and concrete proposals to questions they have never faced before in their history[12].

Are Orthodox women theologians ready to recognize, interpret and discuss these questions? Since the dialogue with the modernity has been difficult in some Orthodox areas, is it possible for them to understand the new facts and ideas: that is, to answer the challenges and ambivalences of post modernity? To give a fair answer, we have to take into account the concrete contexts that Orthodox women grow up and are educated. If we leave out the women of the diaspora, who embrace the Orthodox Tradition consciously and in maturity, many Orthodox women are brought up in societies with a culture deeply influenced by the Orthodox Tradition. This fact makes easier the formation of an "orthodox ethos", but at the same time it includes the danger of the emaciation of the faith.

Some orthodox women accept and respect the influence of Orthodoxy on their cultural identity, but in practice are indifferent to the Orthodox way of life. The lack of good education, correct spiritual guidance, deep and profound understanding of the liturgical texts, substantial pastoral function, understanding of the very essence of the "Church", and the ability to realize the mystery of spiritual experience and to adapt it to the new situation are issues that Orthodox –women and men, lay and clergy– have to discuss. Regarding the necessity of a different model of Orthodox theological education, I agree with Prof. Vassiliadis that "even Orthodox theological institutions, as others around the globe, have been structured in such a way as to educate the 'church' leaders and not the entire people of God... They lost, in

---

12. Pantelis Kalaitzidis, "From the 'Return to the Fathers' to the Need for a Modern Orthodox Theology", *St. Vladimir's Theological Quarterly* 54:1 (2010), p. 5-36.

other words, the *community-centered* and *liturgically-eschatologically-oriented* dimension of theological education"[13].

The presence of an increasing number of Orthodox women who are graduates of theology and other fields of advanced study and who struggle to witness their eucharistic\ecclesial identity and proclaim the real message of the gospel creates a hopeful reality. The faith and the dedication of these women could effectively contribute to the renewal of church life and theological endeavour.

The debate on the role of women in the Orthodox church most often takes place outside the Orthodox communities, that is, Orthodox women in ecumenical relationships. The ecumenical sphere (the EDCSW, the consultations, and the Bossey seminars) helped many Orthodox women to "read" their Tradition more critically and to ask for changes on pastoral issues. This is, of course, one side of the coin. On the other side, we have to admit that there is, still, a kind of "resistance" to the "women's questions" and "feminist theology" in the Orthodox world, which are both perceived as the province of a secular feminism that is destructive of tradition and family[14]. Additionally, in some Orthodox contexts, the term "modernism" and "postmodernism" is commonly understood as an attempt to promote "dogmatic heresy" in the Church. In this frame, women theologians who are seeking contemporary expressions of the ancient faith in their own lives are readily labeled as "feminists" and therefore, automatically,

13. Petros Vassiliadis, "Ecumenical Theological Education: Its Future and Viability", in Eucharist and Witness: *Orthodox Perspectives on the Unity and Mission of the Church*, WCC Publications/Holy Cross Orthodox Press, 1998, p. 109. On women and theological education, see my article "Women in Orthodox Theological Education", in Dietrich Werner, David Esterline, Namsoon Kang & Joshva Raja (eds.), *Handbook of Theological Education in World Christianity*, Regnum Books International, Oxford, 2010, p. 610-14.

14. Leonie Liveris, *Ancient Taboos and Gender Prejudice: Challenges for Orthodox Women and the Church*, Ashagate, Hampshire, 2005, p. xv.

also modernists (or late-modernists) in the most negative sense. Such ideas are widespread not only among the clergy but among many academics as well[15]. In relation to the fact that women in many Orthodox churches were not allowed to go to the seminaries or theological faculties until recently, we understand that we have a long way to go. It is only through education and training that we will fight stereotypes and ideas that are inconvenient with the core message of the gospel. Only through education will the new generation understand better its role in the Church and in the theological process[16].

The book *Women's Voices and Visions of the Church. Reflections of Orthodox Women*, published in 2006 in the frame of the WCC programme "Women's Voices and Visions on Being Church", was an opportunity for orthodox women to write about their participation in Orthodox Church. I will quote two women theologians from that book. The first is Leonie Liveris, well-known among other things for her dissertation, *Ancient Taboos and Gender Prejudice: Challenges for Orthodox Women and the Church*. Liveris asks,

> Can it be too bold, too modern that Orthodox Ecclesiology might begin to re-examine and renew many aspects of church life that do adversely affect the lives of women? Can there not be a new alignment of hierarchy, of including women in decision-making in order to meet the new needs of this century acknowledging many women of faith are competent, qualified and educated and immensely committed to their Orthodox church? Cannot the experiences of women and their knowle-

---

15. Christina Shaheen Reimann, "Orthodox Women in Theological Education", in Kyriaki Karidoyannes FitzGerald (ed.), *Orthodox Women Speak: Discerning the "Signs of the Times*, WCC Publications/Holy Cross Orthodox Press, 1999.
16. Teny Pirri-Simonian, "Authority and Community in the Church: A Personal Reflection", in Christina Breaban, Sophie Deicha, Eleni Kasselouri-Hatzivassiliadi (eds.), *Women's Voices and Visions of the Church: Reflections of Orthodox Women*, WCC Publications, Geneva, 2006, p. 131-35.

dge of contemporary society and family life better inform the church hierarchy?

The second theologian, Teva Regule, points out,

> The Orthodox Church's theology of God and our relationship to Him is life-giving. However, there are times when certain practices in the Church fail to reflect this life-giving theology. One area that has been particularly painful to many girls and women is the practice of only allowing males to serve within the altar in parishes. Although many bishops, priests, and theologians admit that there is no good theological reason for such a practice (women have served in the past as female deacons in Byzantium and as altar servers in Russia and elsewhere as well as in monastic settings), it persists. Within the past few years, a small number of parishes have taken tentative steps to include girls as altar servers. Anecdotal evidence suggests that this has been a welcome development in those settings. It is my fervent hope that this practice, which can have such an important impact on the spiritual development of a young girl, be allowed to continue and grow... We are all called to give glory to God to the best of our abilities within the community of the Church. However, a community whose members are hurt is deformed. We need to be the Church, a therapeutic, healing community. It is then that we can experience the love of God more fully in this world as in the next.

MY CONTEXT: A FEW TIMID STEPS FORWARD?

The Church of Greece (Orthodox) has made few slow but important steps in the direction of empowering the role of women in its life. First of all, the Holy Synod has decided to restore the institution of female deaconate. For the moment, this restoration applies only to nuns within monasteries, but I hope that it will include lay women in the near future. Additionally, the Church of Greece established a special Synodic Commission for women's issues that is working to educate and spiritually support women across Greece. Among its responsibilities is to build an intermetropolitan women's network.

On a theological level, the two Faculties of Theology in Athens and Thessaloniki have included in their curriculum –at undergraduate and post-graduate levels– courses on women's role in Orthodox and Western Christianity. The Volos Academy for Theological Studies dedicated an academic year to the theme "Gender and Religion: The Place of Women in the Church", and published the results of that year in the book by the same name in 2004.

Concerning the dialogue among women of different Christian traditions, two international fora are active in Greece: the European Forum of Christian Women and the European Society of Women in Theological Research. Local groups had the opportunity in 2009 to organize an international conference in Greece (Thessaloniki) and a one-day seminar in Thessaloniki, as well as to publish papers concerning the role of women in Christian communities. But mainly we were able to meet each other, overcome stereotypes and fears, and realize again how important our common confession is in the name of Father, the Son and the Holy Spirit.

CLOSING REMARKS

Returning to the theme of the global ecumenical frame, at the 9th assembly of the World Council of Churches, held in Porto Alegre, Brazil, 14-23 February 2006, Orthodox women were more than visible. We participated as delegates, official observers, lectures, co-opted staff members and stewards. This overwhelming participation of women in the assembly created a feeling of optimism for the future and at the same time a sense of obligation for a sincere self-criticism. Has any progress and change really taken place in the last decades, since the consultations of Agapia (1976) and Rhodes (1988)? Are the changes made sufficient to ensure that progress will continue into the future?

The EDCSW and other programmes, the meetings, the consultations, the Bossey seminars, the publications, and so many other initiatives on international and local level were indeed precious experiences for many Orthodox women around the world. But much remains to be done!

The creation of a world Orthodox women's network for example is still an unfulfilled dream. Such a network would permit a fruitful cooperation, an exchange of information on Orthodox theological research; it would provide a forum for exploring common creative ways our contemporary concerns and proposals modify, reform and convert church practices and attitudes. This was, is and always will be a necessity because,

"Many women were also there ... " (Mt. 27:55):

> Faithful to the Lord just from the beginning... from village to village... from the Temple to the Cross... from the Cross to the empty Tomb... Many women are still there... faithful to His vision, teaching and mission: an eucharistic, inclusive, just, full of care and love community.

THE ESSENTIALS OF THEOLOGY IN FEMINIST –THAT IS TO SAY ECCLESIAL– PERSPECTIVE

Spyridoula Athanasopoulou-Kypriou

The purpose of this brief theological comment is threefold. First, I would like to suggest that we, namely the members of the Church regardless of what we are, should re-examine the essentials of theology understood as dogmatics. Through this, we will stress this time the importance of divine revelation –that is to say, the theological character of theology– and explain why by stressing the otherness of God and the fact that revelation is Christian theology's foundation, we can overcome the problem of "objectification". Second, I want to maintain that in a truly ecclesial context – one which respects both the ontological difference between the uncreated God and his (is God really a he?) creatures and the fact that all human beings are unique in such a way that we cannot speak of a universal spirituality valid for all times and all people – nobody can be excluded from the making of theology. Thus, everybody's spirituality matters. Third, I will attempt to explain why we –that is, the Orthodox– should not be afraid or suspicious of the term "feminist" and its connotations. This is especially the case if we want to develop a praxis-based theology that will be true to the ecclesiological principle that makes clear that the Church is all inclusive, cares for everybody, remains forever a stranger within history, and always seeks the end times since her being resides in the kingdom of God.

At this point, one would rightly ask why maintaining the theological character of theology is related to women's issues, which is the subject of this meeting in Volos. Stressing the otherness of God and the fact that revelation alone is Christian theology's foundation is directly related to the problem of "objectification". "Objectification" is associated with feminist theory and especially the work of Catharine MacKinnon and Andrea Dworkin who claimed that (sexual) objectification determines the lives of women to the extent that they (women) can think of themselves only as objects[1]. In other words, the more I see you (and treat you) as an object, the more you are convinced that you are one. When I objectify you, I use you and I do not recognize that you are a subject different from me and with very different feelings and experiences that I must respect. Even when I say "I love you", I subjugate you or consume you. I take you for a direct object, I order you, I prescribe this for you, and I subject you to these truths, to this order. For Luce Irigaray,

> I love you, I desire you, I take you, I seduce you, I order you, I instruct you, and so on, always risk annihilating the alterity of the other, of transforming him/her into my property, my object, of reducing him/her to what is mine, into mine, meaning what is already a part of my field of existential or material properties[2].

In terms of ethics and morality, objectifying you is tantamount to using you and abusing you, alienating your (that is the other's) freedom in my subjectivity, my world, my language.

In terms of epistemology, objectification assumes a certain methodology of knowing something, be it a fe/male human being or not. Whatever is to be known, it is considered separate from the knower. The knower is the subject who takes the initiative to know something that is turned into an object, and hence when it is ready to be known by the knower, this thing is objectified. Knower's may employ their rea-

---

1. See Catharine MacKinnon, *Feminism Unmodified*, Harvard University Press, Cambridge, MA, 1987; *Toward a Feminist Theory of State*, Harvard University Press, Cambridge, MA, 1989; Andrea Dworkin, *Intercourse*, The Free Press, New York, 1987; and the chapter on "Objectification" in Martha Nussbaum, *Sex and Social Justice*, Oxford University Press, 1999.
2. Luce Irigaray, *I Love To You: A Sketch for a Felicity Within History*, trans. Alison Martin, Routledge, New York and London, 1996, p.110.

son or their senses or both in order to examine their object. The main purpose of objectification is to know something by defining what it is in terms of certain properties and qualities (age, color, nationality, weight, psychological state etc.). By identifying something, I control it. I can identify something in such a way that it can serve my needs. For example, I could identify women as tender and therefore more suitable for staying at home to bring up their children. Or I could identify God as benevolent and therefore willing to forgive me for being violent to my wife. When I objectify something, not only do I see it as a commodity but I also imprison it in my own representation.

In terms of Christian theology, I objectify God when I treat God as something that can be known by my reason or senses or by both. When I objectify God, theology becomes theology because instead of referring to God, it refers to our human logos (reason and language). Yet, as I said earlier, revelation alone is the foundation of Christian theology. Stressing the importance of divine revelation marks a shift from treating God (the ultimately Other since God is uncreated and we are created) as an object to treating God as a person. If we respect the otherness of God, we do not objectify the divine and priority is given to God's self-disclosure as love in the person of Christ. True theology, as Jean-Luc Marion claims, is focused iconically on God's excessive self-revelation as love (God's self-disclosure as agape) (1 Jn 4:8) and needs: i) to abandon a metaphysical understanding of God in terms of being and ii) to reject the authority of reason (not reject reason altogether), which is only capable of thinking in terms of the categories and properties of being[3]. Logos/reason very often attempts to control everything; it regulates and puts everything in an order that can be an arbitrary order. It does this through repetition

---

3. Jean-Luc Marion, *God Without Being*, trans. Thomas A. Carlson, University of Chicago Press, Chicago and London, 1991. In this book, Marion develops the idea that reason is capable of thinking of God in terms of Being but if we start worshipping Being as God then we would be worshipping an idol.

and standardization, and hence we (Christians) have ended up with standard textbooks of dogmatic theology that everyone recognizes; for example, we have ended up with standard –that is, stereotypical– representations of wo/men that remain unquestionable. But beliefs and representations that are formed by human reason alone are not reliable, let alone unquestionable.

Gregory of Nyssa seems to suggest that the reliability of our beliefs and representations depend on love. The idea that love is a necessary condition of knowledge is expressed in the eighth homily on Ecclesiastes,

> The inner disposition towards what is desired, functioning through pleasure and passionate feeling, produces love; ... The place we are drawn to by affection is the one we adapt our souls to... Whether the disposition of the soul is towards good or evil, the object of affection infiltrates the soul[4].

According to Gregory's understanding of the "knowing process", the soul familiarizes herself with what she loves. This familiarization, as the Greek verb *oikeioumai* suggests, involves two things: first, the soul's becoming like what she loves, in which case the soul gets identified with the beloved thing/entity, and second, the soul's becoming familiar with the beloved thing/entity, in which case the soul progresses in knowledge.

For Gregory, then, we cannot know unless we love. Although we can form beliefs about the world, other beings and God, it is only if these beliefs are produced by a loving person that they become knowledge and are reliable. Love confers reliability to the agent's beliefs because, first, her beliefs are not accidental, the agent being responsible for her disposition of love, and second, the agent, who respects the alterity of

---

4. George Stuart Hall (ed.), *Gregory of Nyssa Homilies on Ecclesiastes: An English Version with Supporting Studies*, Walter de Gruyter, Berlin and New York, 1993, p. 129.

the things/entities she wants to know and opens herself to them, allows the entities/things to reveal their properties and attributes.

As Gregory seems to claim in the sixth homily on the beatitudes, people can form beliefs about the visible world, but these beliefs are reliable when they are formed by loving people who have first opened themselves to the things/entities in order for the things/entities to grant them with their presence within their soul[5]. Gregory does consider the intellect/reason as being central in the process of knowing something, for instance the divine, and as able to form true beliefs, that is, beliefs that correspond to reality. However, he suggests that the true beliefs formed by the intellect/reason alone become knowledge only if they are not formed accidentally but are products of a reliable loving person who has introspective access to their formation. Moreover, the reliability of beliefs depends upon the way a belief is formed. Love confers reliability to beliefs because when a belief is formed by means of love, then the process followed in obtaining that belief is reliable. The process now is reliable because, first, the subject opens herself to things/entities so that she can experience the presence of them in her soul; and second, the subject employs all the sources of knowledge (perception, memory, consciousness, reason and testimony) in order to become like the things/entities and thus make herself familiar with them.

The fact that love is a necessary condition of knowledge does not mean that when we love we cannot be deceived. For Gregory, love does not make the loving agent infallible. Rather, love enables the agent to know partially. When Gregory takes love as epistemically valuable, he assumes first that the essence of everything is incomprehensible; second that human knowledge has limits; and finally that knowledge is an ongoing process[6]. If, on the one hand, love is a condition of know-

---

5. Gregory of Nyssa, *Orationes VIII de Beatitudibus*, MPG 44, 1264-1276.
6. Commenting on the incomprehensibility of the essence of anything, Gregory writes that whosoever searches the whole of revelation will find therein no doctrine

ledge and, on the other, knowledge is understood as an ongoing process that is never completed, then the only way to advance our knowledge is by continuing to love, by transcending the partial knowledge we have in order to make further discovery, and by respecting the otherness/alterity of all the things/entities to be known. Thus, mistakes may occur and loving agents can be deceived because of human limitations. However, love has a corrective operation. Think, for instance, of the history of science. Theories are constantly being replaced by new ones because scientists continue to open themselves to the world and employ all the available sources of justification and knowledge. Mistakes have been spotted because some scientists, driven by their love for the world, did not believe that knowledge could be complete and continued researching[7].

Love is epistemically valuable and has a corrective operation only when by loving we don't objectify the beloved other, be it God or not, and we maintain a relation of indirection with the beloved things respecting their alterity/otherness. The feminist philosopher Luce Iri-

---

of the divine nature, nor indeed of anything else that has a substantial existence. For, as he believes, we are ignorant of everything, including of ourselves (*Contra Eunomium*, in W. Jaeger (ed.), *Gregorii Nysseni opera*, Vols. 1.1 & 2.2, Brill, Leiden, 1960, bk. 2, ch. 1, sections 106-107). To express also the idea that knowledge is an ongoing process, Gregory employs the term "epectasis" (ἐπέκτασις=ἐπι+ἐκ+τασις= expansion, extension). On the one hand, as the prefix "ἐπί" (meaning "at" or "towards") gives evidence, the word expresses the idea that there is knowledge of the things/entities. The soul is, in a true sense, identified with whatever she wants to know. On the other hand, things/entities remain transcendent and are thus constantly beyond. As a result, the soul must always go out of herself (prefix "ἐκ"="out of"), transcending the knowledge she has acquired to make further discovery.

7. The ideas about Gregory's understanding of love as epistemically valuable and his insight of the knowing process are taken from Penelope Voutsina & Spyridoula Athanasopoulou-Kypriou, "The 'Illuminating' Value of Love: Gregory of Nyssa's Understanding of Love as Epistemically Valuable and Love's Contribution to Virtue Epistemology", *Philotheos* 5 (2005), p. 248-54.

garay transforms the transitive French verb "aimer", to love or to like, into an intransitive verb (a verb not requiring a direct object). Irigaray intends the potential (O)other to be positioned as subject and not object and introduces the preposition "to" (à) to separate the potential "you" of the I love you from the action of the "I". Thus, I love you becomes I love to you.

> I love to you means I do not subjugate you or consume you. I respect you (as irreducible)... The "to" is the sign of non-immediacy, of mediation between us... The "to" is also a barrier against alienating the other's freedom in my subjectivity, my world, my language. I love to you thus means: I do not take you for a direct object, nor for an indirect object by revolving around you[8].

With the phrase I love to you, we attempt to have two subjects (and not a subject objectifying the (O)other) in a loving relationship.

In terms of Zizioulas's insight of patristic thought about the fall and sin, "the fall consists in the refusal to make being dependent on communion, in a rupture between truth and communion"[9]. Thus, in a Christian context, sin is to be understood as "objectification". When there is rapture between truth and communion, then the truth of being acquires priority over the truth of communion, truth precedes communion and knowledge precedes love. As Zizioulas explains, "this is natural for created existence", for when the created (the given) world posits its being ultimately with reference to itself and not to an uncreated being (God), the substance of things becomes the ultimate content of truth[10]. If I refuse to make being dependent on communion, it means that communion is no longer constitutive of being,

---

8. Luce Irigaray, *I Love To You*, p. 9-10.
9. John D. Zizioulas, *Being as Communion: Studies in Personhood and the Church*, Darton, Longman and Todd, London, 1985, p. 102.
10. Ibid.

for truth is constitutive of being and thus the being of things must be recognized before a relationship can take place.

> Thus the world consists of objects, of things whose ontological status one has to recognize before one can relate to them. The truth of these "objects" becomes, therefore, a provocation for the knower; the known and the knower exist as two opposite partners;... the subject and the object constitute a pair whose presence determines epistemology... In associating truth with the nature of things... man [sic] restricts himself to reaching a relationship between communion and love only after obtaining a knowledge of the "object" of his love. The "other", whether in the form of a "person" or a "thing", is present as an object of knowledge [and not as a subject in a mutually loving relationship] before any relationship of communion can take place[11].

The only alternative to objectification would be, as Zisioulas proposes, to make communion constitutive of being, but in this case a denial of the fall, redemption from it and a savior would be implied[12]. God reveals the truth in the person of Christ. Christ is the truth and truth is communion and love. Christ is the revelation of true personhood for in his person being and communion (love) coincide[13]. For human beings to see the world, things and other human beings as Christ does—that is, not as objects but as subjects worth loving before knowing them—a new birth in the Spirit is required so that each baptized person can herself become "Christ"[14].

The feminist rejection of objectification and the respect of the other's otherness that is so well expressed with the phrase I love to you assume an ontology of otherness and personhood that gives ontological

11. Ibid., p. 102-04.
12. Ibid., p. 102.
13. Ibid., p. 107.
14. Ibid., p. 113.

priority to love and personhood. In terms of an ontology of otherness and personhood, it is not important to speak or think the truth but to "do the truth" (John 3:21)[15]. That is why I think it is more important, and thus more difficult, acting (making, doing, fighting for, performing) equality and justice than speaking of them.

Crucial for our making of theology are the following: arguing for an ontology of personhood and against the objectification of the (O) other; respecting the alterity of others and especially the Otherness of the divine and the ontological gulf between the uncreated and the created; realizing that "God is Love" not only in the sense of God's self-disclosure as love in the person of Christ but also in the sense of God's loving before being (since the cause of the Trinity is the love of the person of the Father); and "doing the truth" instead of objectifying the others in order to know the truth. These are crucial for our referring, our speaking about God to communion with God. If we take the above into consideration, then certain practices would change.

For instance, in terms of an ontology of personhood as developed by Zizioulas, priority is given to "who" one is and not to "what" one is[16]. The important thing about women, homosexuals, people of color or with disabilities etc. is that they are persons with names and not that they have certain properties. Everybody's experience matters, everybody's suffering matters, everybody is saved in Christ. Nobody can be excluded, as nobody's experience can be considered less important on the basis of a human property, for to exclude someone on this basis is to reject the "other". A person (always embodied) is important regardless of the gender that is the cause of division (male-female). The particularity of each person is secured ontologically. All this calls for

15. Needless to say, we owe much to the work of John Zizioulas for developing the theological prerequisites for ontology of otherness and for constructing an ontology of personhood based on the person of the Father who is the cause of the Trinity.

16. John D. Zizioulas, *Communion and Otherness*, T and T Clark, London and New York, 2006, p. 110.

a reconsideration of the concept of love. As Zizioulas puts it, "Love is not a feeling or disposition of the 'self' towards an 'other'"[17], as it is when I say, "I love you". "Rather, it is a gift coming from the 'other' as an affirmation of one's uniqueness in an indispensable relation through which one's particularity is secured ontologically"[18]. When I say I love to you, I try to express that "love is the assertion that one exists as 'other', that is, particular and unique, in relation to some 'other' who affirms him or her as 'other'. In love, relation generates otherness; it does not threaten it;"[19] nor does otherness dissolve in sameness through communion. So in order not to have one voice – an authoritarian male voice speaking on behalf of everybody and thus silencing other voices by reducing otherness to sameness – we need to listen to a range of different voices, respect everyone's spirituality (respecting thus the Holy Spirit), sympathize with the other, and not feel fear of diversity, for "perfect love casts out fear" (1 Jn 4:18)[20].

Yet voices that have been silenced for so long may not know how to speak. They may not know the conventions that make us speak with one voice – that is, with the dominant voice, the voice that has the power to speak. New questions need to be asked, old teachings need to be phrased differently in order to convey the message to everybody. Old oppressive customs that affect not just women but all those who don't comply with the cultural norm, need to be recon-

---

17. Ibid., p. 55.

18. Ibid.

19. Ibid.

20. "Christianity has historically been blind to questions of gender believing that 'mankind' includes the experiences of women and men and encompasses all that makes us human. This assumption of course works in many ways, to a certain extent it becomes self-fulfilling in that women do begin to understand themselves through the male lens and in so many respects begin to see themselves as defective, insufficient or as simply experientially deluded" (Marcella Althaus-Reid & Lisa Isherwood, *Controversies in Feminist Theology*, SCM, London, 2007, p. 18).

sidered and not justified in the name of Tradition; for according to what is called "Christian Tradition", culture is well blurred with God's self-revelation as love in the person of Christ. In other words, the essentials of theology need to be considered time and time again so that we, the ecclesial body that does not exclude anybody, can safeguard the theological character of theology – that is, the Christian character of theology – and not end up worshipping idols, the logoi of our created mind and our traditional customs.

In the end, if we don't want to worship a systematic theology with a homogenous agenda that excludes people's experiences and has a hierarchical and oppressive set of priorities, the call could be twofold. First, we should disrupt the structures of sin (very often linked to women) and the thematic organization of the key themes for theological reflection   reminding us of a theistic and scholastic theology. Second, we should continue to produce an increasingly a-systematic theology that may allow new questions and different sorts of interrogations to take place among different theological subjects from all over the world – and especially from developing world margins of theological power[21].

Elisabeth Behr-Sigel is very critical of the Orthodox Church's refusal to take part in the questionings of "feminist" theology under the pretext that feminine perspectives in Christian faith are an alien concept to Orthodox women. In other words, Behr-Siger refuses to take the idea of women's ignorance of feminist theology as normative. As she puts it,

---

21. Cf., I bid., p. 15. The Orthodox theologian C. Agoras warns us against an ecclesial theology that descends to being an idol; that is to say, a closed systematic theology that doesn't refer to God and cannot be named Christian (C. Agoras, "Fysi kai prosopo, historia kai eschata ston Pergamou Ioanni (Zizioula) kais ton Christo Yannara" in P. Kalaitzidis et al., eds, *Anatarakseis sti Metapolemiki Theologia: I Theologia tou '60*, (in Greek) Indiktos, Athens, 2009, p. 209-10).

> If this [feminist theology being an alien concept to Orthodox women] refers to a simple statement of phenomenological and sociological order, I agree with this, but not if it reckons to express a rule as "absolute". Many Orthodox women, in fact, ignore these researches, that seem to them to be strange and foreign. But, like my friend Metropolitan Anthony of Sourozh, I want them to know about them, to assimilate them in order to be able, eventually, to evangelize them and also, thanks to them, to evangelize the historical social dimension of our church[22].

Although Behr-Sigel encourages women to know about the questionings of feminist theology, Orthodox women face a less encouraging reality. Speaking her own mind, using her own voice, an Orthodox woman speaks her truth. Leonie Liveris writes,

> As an Orthodox woman in the late twentieth century I also seek to find a voice and complete the circle for my church to be made inclusive and whole. It is clear to me that no matter that we acknowledge how holy and learned the church fathers are, too often their advice, authority, androcentric clericalism and misogyny reveal that the voices of men cannot always respond to my questions as a woman of my time. They do not have all the answers, for their experiences and external influences combined with an ignorance of biology and the full nature of women[23].

At this point, we have to realize that although feminism used to be a project primarily for women, feminism is now for everybody. Respe-

---

22. Elisabeth Behr-Sigel, "Feminine Images and Orthodox spirituality", *Ecumenical Review* 60.1-2 (2008), p. 14.

23. Leonie B. Liveris, "Authority in the Church as the Body of Christ: The Orthodox Vision", *Ecumenical Review* 60.1-2 (2008), p. 107.

cting all human persons (who are all different subjects that shouldn't be objectified), caring for and including everybody (male or female, old or young, white or black, able-bodied or with a disability) with their experiences and spirituality, arguing against oppression and for equality are part of the contemporary feminist agenda. Feminism started as a struggle for equality but it has now become a struggle for the right to be different. Christian ecclesiology is based on ideas and teachings very similar to those of feminist thought and shares with feminism similar aspirations. Following the Bible, Orthodox theologians have stressed that the nature of ecclesia is all-inclusive; all-embracing; against power relations and oppression; and for equality, peace and justice (cf Gal. 3:28; Gal. 4:24; 1 Cor. 12)[24]. In an analogous way, feminism yearns for inclusivity and equality and fights oppression and unjust hierarchies.

One could note that ecclesiology not only shares the same principles and aspirations with feminism but is also critical of the world in the way that feminism is. As Zizioulas points out, "The Church is constantly in a situation, not of identifying with History, but on the contrary, in a crisis situation with History"[25]. One could argue that with respect to their attitude towards the world, ecclesiology and feminism share the same purpose, which is to make this world a better place. Yet this is only true to the extent that ecclesia is expected to help anybody in need, being philanthropic by definition. For there is a crucial difference between ecclesiology and feminism as a political movement: "The task of the former is to bring to its completion the

24. For the metaphorical depictions of the church that point to her all embracing and loving nature see Dimitra Koukoura, "The Church According to the Orthodox Tradition and Its Metaphorical Imagery", in Christina Breaban, Sophie Deicha, Eleni Kasselouri-Hatzivassiliadi (eds.), *Women's Voices and Visions of the Church: Reflections of Orthodox Women*, WCC Publications, Geneva, 2006, p. 9-29.
25. John D. Zizioulas, "The Structure and the Organizing of the Church", *Orthodox Outlook for Dogmatic Enquiries*, at: http://www.oodegr.com/english/dogmatiki1/

eschaton that has been inaugurated within it, while the latter claims to improve the life of the citizens"[26].

Despite the crucial difference between feminism and ecclesiology, I suggest that we as Orthodox wo/men should not be afraid of the term "feminist". For in order for our perspective to be truly ecclesial, it has to be feminist in a way. This is why I disagree with those theologians who are very reluctant to use the term. Moreover, refusing to deal with the questions raised by feminist theology is a way of silencing the voice of the others: effectively warning them that if they ever deal with gender issues (let alone "feminist" issues) their future (academic or otherwise) is in danger. To claim that Orthodox women don't need feminist theology because the icons of the Mother of God are an indication that the Orthodox church is not misogynist, or that the ordination of women in the Orthodox church is not an issue for Orthodox women, or that women who are challenging male authority in the

---

26. Tamara Grdzelidze, "A Theological Reflection on Being the Church", in Christina Breaban, Sophie Deicha, Eleni Kasselouri-Hatzivassiliadi (eds.), *Women's Voices and Visions of the Church*, p. 58. Speaking of the eschatological perspective of ecclesia, Zizioulas writes, "That is where the true Being of the Church is; not in that which the Church is presently, in History, but in that eschatological form which is to be revealed. Her true identity therefore is there; the Church is by Her nature the community of the Time to come, or in other words, the Kingdom of God, and Her organization must necessarily reflect that eschatological hypostasis of Hers... That is also why the Church cannot, by nature, ever find Her expression amongst secular, historical realities with which She will more or less always find Herself in a certain dialectic situation, regardless how many times She encounters them; She will always be in a conflicting relationship with them. Consequently, the Church cannot be transformed into a State; She cannot be expressed by a political party. She cannot coincide with a particular social structure or organization... The Church can never be identified –and never should be– with Historical realities, because She is the image of the eschatological community... the way in which the Church materializes this image in Herself is only through the Sacraments of the Church, and especially in the Divine Eucharist" (Op. cit.,"The Structure and the Organizing of the Church").

Church are actually attracted by the power themselves, are all ways of discouraging women from thinking of questioning the patriarchical and oppressive elements of their tradition.

I consider the feminist perspective very useful when considering the essentials of *theo*logy with respect to God's self-disclosure as love and communion in the person of Christ. We should keep a feminist –that is to say, an all-inclusive and loving– perspective if we want to struggle for the church "to become a little more of what it is in the mind of our God, One in three persons: a community, or rather a communion of persons in his likeness, men and women ineffably different but equal in dignity, free and responsible, under the inspiration of the Holy Spirit"[27]. Moreover, I argue for the importance of the term "feminist", for it reminds us all that there is still a women's cause. Equality, social justice, peace and respect for differences are not historical realities and we need a term to remind us of this ongoing reality. In other words, we need a term to remind us of the eschatological perspective of theology and, for that matter, of the eschatological character of ecclesiology.

Finally, some claim that feminist discourse is passé, which is another way to intimidate people who are trying to be different. Yet in so far as feminist discourse argues for and feminist activism struggles for the right to be different and not just equal, then feminist discourse has a future. In other words, if we are to develop a praxis-based theology, a theology of servitude and a theology of otherness, we should adopt a feminist perspective and its aporetic and challenging stance towards this world.

27. Behr-Sigel, "Feminine Images and Orthodox Spirituality", p. 7.

MOTIVATIONAL THOUGHTS ON FEMINIST THEOLOGY: A DEMAND TO HARMONIZE THEOLOGICAL TRADITION WITH ECCLESIASTICAL PRACTICE (WITH REGARD TO THE PARTICIPATION OF ORTHODOX WOMEN IN THE ECUMENICAL MOVEMENT)

ANASTASIA GKITSI

Feminist theology was born and raised in Western, not Eastern Orthodox, societies. Does this fact mean that the latter relies on already established and unwieldy –or even worse, fire-proof– institutes and institutional forms that have no desire for modernity and readjustment? Or has the Eastern Orthodox tradition marched through the course of history without the need for such changes, never having experienced the subordination of the female element and person during the last centuries? Even if we suppose this subordination has never been felt throughout the past milleniums, does Orthodoxy still insist on declaring that the parity it evangelizes –which, hermeneutically, is theologically grounded on hagiographic[1] and some patristic texts[2]– is satisfactorily expressed in the existing concrete social and ecclesiastical condition of woman nowadays?

I would be reassured if I could at the outset answer the above questions affirmatively, stating that the position of woman in the Orthodox church has been in both theory and practice equivalent to that of man. These are questions that have troubled me for many years now. They arose when I first made contact with a Protestant German woman in my first year of post-graduate study in Geneva who asked me, "Don't you feel that your church degrades you by depriving you

---

1. Gen. 1: 27 "... and God created man, He did so in His image, male and female He created them".

2. Gregory the Theologian LZ' 6, PG 36, 289A: "One is the creator of man and woman, they were both made of the same dust, according to the same image, and they have one law, one death, one resurrection".

of the right to practice priesthood?" My answer was spontaneous, like an ancient legacy of experience or a feeling that I had never doubted; maybe because until then I had never considered the fact that the blessing, as well as the great weight of responsibility, for the special priesthood that – according to ecclesiastical rules – is only carried by male clergy in the Orthodox church to be a sign of degradation.

However, if you want to be honest with the one you are in dialogue with, and intend to meet with him/her and not – as usually happens– fall into parallel monologues, caricatures of dialogue, first you have to be honest with yourself. I believe that this is the only way that a fruitful and effective dialogue can take place. And for people to be honest with themselves, they have to separate their thought of the ideal[3] from the real;[4] to appreciate and estimate these anew, so that they will finally be able to reconstruct and adjust them according to new data. In simple words, they shall have to separate that which is and seems to be theologically perfect (which is realized only under particular conditions and with specific actions) from that which is real (which exists as it is and can be accounted for through statistical evidence)[5].

Therefore, for the Orthodox church to enter into a truly honest dialogue with other confessions and religions, it first has to realize its character anew, which, in its aggregating, eucharistic and eschatological way, promotes the parity[6] of the genders. Once it has

3. The equal, fair, peaceful society is the one that is eschatologically revealed in the great mystery of the divine Eucharist.

4. Human society experiences violence, division and discrimination on every level (racial, cultural, national, linguistic, religious, social etc.).

5. Unemployment, wage inequality, immigration, sexual abuse, difficulty in professional development, all forms of violence, psychological coercion, perpetuation of erroneous perceptions about the inferiority of women etc.

6. I prefer the term "parity" to "equality" as I think it renders better the respect towards the special charisms and characteristics of the two genders as well as maintaining the difference in their personal features.

realized this character, the Orthodox church should try to act on it. No contradiction should exist between the Orthodox Tradition that intends woman to be lacking in nothing compared to man and the daily ecclesiastical practice that attests to woman's degraded position. This position is due to the preservation of canons and benedictions that are opposed to both the philanthropic spirit of Jesus and the democratic spirit of human rights.

The eschatological prospect of the Orthodox church prompts it to a continuous incarnation and an everlasting centralization of its theological word in the social matrix of each era. Because of its eschatological hypostasis, the Church (clergy and laity) must reform –or even transform where it is possible– the historical conditions and the social reality by redefining the value of the human person, which overcomes every racial, cultural, and social discrimination and difference. According to the words of the Apostle of the Nations, "There is neither Jew nor Greek, neither slave nor free man, neither male nor female; because you are all one in Jesus Christ"[7].

Christ himself was a "scandalous"[8] and controversial figure in his time, fiercely attacking typolatry and the complacent conscience that accepts injustice. So the Church (laity and clergy) in a mimetic way – and with the profound faith that the Holy Spirit still exists and continues to spread its grace – must also take action that embodies the truth and vision of the Holy Spirit in the historical communities which it guides. The change in the Orthodox church does not have the tone of modernity or of an external parasitical formation, but has the boldness to revive forgotten ecclesiastical practices;[9] practices

---

7. Many are the Fathers who, based on these words, ground theologically both the ontological equality and the clear functional difference of the two genders. See Basil the Great and John Chrysostom.

8. John 8: 3-4: "Let the one of you who is sinless first throw a stone against her".

9. Such as, for instance, the institute of Deaconesses as attested in Rom. 16: 1-2, which has been a special order of diaconic priesthood corresponding to that of deacons. However, as time went by it fell into obscurity and finally became obsolete,

that have been buried under the relentless historical prevalence of patriarchal hierarchy.

The feminist movement – wherever it comes from[10], on whatever reasons it is grounded[11], whichever Christian confessions[12] it is identified with – can become a god-sent opportunity for the Orthodox church to rest the souls of a great part of its flock[13]. In this way, it will prove the "hypostatic" character of its pastoral care[14] for each believer, man and woman.

And, of course, when we talk of change in the Orthodox church we do not necessarily mean the reckless – and, perhaps, externally imposed – consent to practices that are either inconsistent with or disapproved by the Church itself[15] during its course in history. Mainly, we mean the open discussion of issues[16] which, as long as they remain

with the exception of some rare cases.

10. Feminist theology was developed in America with the ground-breaking book by Elizabeth Cady Stanton, *Women's Bible*. For further analysis on this subject see Evanthia Adamtziloglou, *Woman in Pauline Theology: Hermeneutic Analysis of A, Cor. 11, 2-16*, Thessaloniki, 1989, p. 59-78 (in Greek); Eleni Kasselouri-Hatzivassiliadi, *Feminist Hermeneutics: The "Gender" Factor in Modern Biblical Hermeneutics*, P. Pournaras, Thessaloniki, 2003 (in Greek).

11. At the beginning of the movement, the reasons were social, political, and financial, but not theological.

12. See liberating movements, products of Western Christianity.

13. The participation of women in the ecclesiastical act is by far greater than that of men.

14. "Hypostatic" in the sense that it refers to the human person; it aims to heal a specific person, and that is why it cannot be generalized.

15. In the Orthodox Church, the forbiddance of women's ordination in the upper clergy has no theological backing. However, we can by no means overlook or lightheartedly discredit the avoidance of the church since the beginning of its formation to follow due course. See Yokarini Constantinou, *Women's Ordination in the Frame of the Ecumenical Movement*, Epektasi, Katerini, 1995.

16. Such issues are women's ordination, the reintroduction of the deaconesses, the forbidding of women to enter the holy altar, the forty-days benedictions, involuntary miscarriage, body impurity etc.

unresolved, damage the internal dynamics of the Church as much as its external dynamics. The internal damage is manifested in the fact that it gives the clergy and the laity (mainly women) the sad impression of controversial divided action (theological and ecclesiastical or theory and practice) and of complacency (with the emaciated letter) over contradictory/revolutionary spirit (of Jesus). On the other hand, its dynamic projection and significant contribution to the world are weakened –mainly over ecumenical fermentations– as its practice is not presented in accordance with its theology. Thus, its word proves to be unreliable.

The Orthodox church has a rich supply of female forms, with Virgin Mary as the most prominent and honored one. There is an equal number of male and female saints and martyrs on the church calendar, a dynamic presence of spiritual women in monasticism, and a tender poetic woman's voice in the church hymnology[17]. The Church also has the common women of faith, who keep intact the female quality of offering mercy and love and who act voluntarily and piously, in this way practicing the general priesthood. Finally, the Orthodox church has that dynamic prospect that can make "the good alteration" happen both for each person individually and in the society that surrounds them, even if this has to take place under adverse historical conditions.

---

17. Nuns Martha, Theodosia, Thekla and Kassiani were excellent hymnographs. The hymnographic work of Kassiani became part of the Orthodox Church Hymnology: a) *Magnificat* of Christmas Vespers, "When Augustus was monarch on earth…"; b) *Idiomelon Liti* of Annunciation, "Angel Gabriel was sent"; c) Magnificat of Aposticha of the G. Wednesday Orthros, "Woman has fallen in many sins"; d) Hirmoi of the Great Sabbath canon, "On the sea wave".

THE ISSUE OF FEMALE ORDINATION/PRIESTHOOD IN THE ECUMENICAL AND INTER-ORTHODOX DISCUSSION

Natallia Vasilevich

The issue of female ordination was raised not in the framework of the feminist movement nor through the introduction of other confessions. Rather, it was raised through the internal necessity of the Orthodox church for additional ministries in special contexts. In these, the ordained female could help her male co-minister in interaction with lay women in performing a wide range of social, missionary, and educational roles – and also a liturgical role, though different from the male, ordained ministries.

In the Orthodox church of Russia, the discussion on reviving the order of deaconess started in the first part of the 19th century, during the governance of St Metropolitan Philaret (Drozdov) of Moscow, one of the prominent church figures of the synodical period. Research indicates that there could have been some influence of Western Protestant congregations, but this was not a determining influence. In the 1830s, the first to make an appeal to church authorities to revive the order of diaconate for female missionaries was the famous missionary, St Archimandrite Makarios (Gluharev), head of Altai mission in Siberia (1830-43). He received a negative response from Metropolitan Philaret, who argued that it was not a coincidence that this order ceased in the church and that it was justified by Tradition.

Such an *argumentum ad traditio* can be used on the issue of deaconesses by both supporters and opponents equally. On the one hand, the diaconal ministry of females had a long-standing history in the first centuries of the Christian Church; on the other hand, it completely ceased and the last centuries of Tradition have been of exclusively male ministries in the Church. Still, in 1837-38, Archimandrite Makarios's above-mentioned proposal in his project of missionary reform also included a statute for deaconesses to work for the mission. This proposal was re-issued several times, and in 1894 was published as a book[1]. The deaconesses in missionary work was later also expressed by St Nicolas (Kassatkin) of Japan[2]. Metropolitan Philaret himself was influenced by the ideas of Archimandrite Makarios and although he did not support the revival of female diaconate in general, he ordained hiegumenia Maria (Tuchkova) in a diaconic rite in 1840 in Moscow, testimonies of which can be found in some publications, for example in Nadiezhda Paglazova[3]. In this case, when diaconic ordination was undertaken as a particular act and for a monastic female, we can also recall St Metropolitan Nectarios (Kephalas) of Pentapolis who ordained two females in the diaconic order in 1911; although it was ad hoc ordination that cannot be extended to a more general context, still, both examples give precedence and are referred to.

Except Gluharev, the will for a revival of the female diaconate was expressed by a Petersburg priest, Alexander Gumilevsky, who proposed a new statute for the communities of sisters of charity (founded by the great duchess, Elena Pavlovna) as deaconesses. These, according to him, were more in accordance with Orthodox Tradition, and he also proposed special vestments with diaconic orarion[4]. According to Karpycheva, the emperor commented on this project by stating that these "new types of ministeries... would not be understandable for

1. Макарий (Глухарев), архим. Мысли о способах к успешнейшему распространению христианской веры между евреями, магометанами и язычниками в Российской державе. - М., 1894.

2. Николай (Касаткин), архим. Воззвание Японской духовной миссии к Русской Церкви. // Миссионер, 1876, №21, стр. 169.

3. Паглазова Н. Святитель Филарет Московский и две попытки восстановления чина дьяконисс в Русской церкви его времени. - Личность в Церкви и обществе = Материалы Международной научно-богословской конференции, 17-19 сентября 2001 г. - С. 240 - 256.

4. С – ов [Скроботов]. Приходской священник Александр Васильевич Гумилевский. СПб., 1871.

the majority [and] shouldn't be invented"[5]. This argumentation *ad populum* –the people will not accept it, the people will not understand something new– is quite widespread in discussion on any change in the Church, even minor changes. The reception by the people is used as a very important ecclesial argument, while the motivation of the people is not taken in consideration. Russia has a prominent example of such "non-reception" of a new rite, which led many people into the schism of "old-believers"– a very painful issue for quite a long period of time.

This does not mean that the Russian Church was not ready for reforms. On the contrary, during the preparation for the Council 1917-1918, many issues were raised in a very sharp and sometimes radical way; even now, many of the statements sound revolutionary. The issue of the female diaconate was not an exception. Already during preconciliar time, several works on deaconesses were published; the issue was discussed in ecclesial periodicals and in preconciliar commissions; and the introduction of this ministry was supported by prominent theologians, hierarchs, wide circles of church people, members of the royal family, and leaders of female lay and monastic communities.

The following works of that time are just a few: *Deaconesses of the Ancient Church* by Maslov[6], *Deaconesses of the First Centuries of Christianity* by P.E.[7], *Deaconesses of the First Centuries of Christianity* by Dobroravov[8], and *Deaconesses in the Orthodox Church* by Troitsky[9].

5. Карпычева Л.А. Общины сестер милосердия и православная церковь. - http://www.omophor.ru/articles/sistercommunity.htm#_ednref41

6. Маслов И.. Диакониссы древней церкви // Дух христианина I отдел, январь, Спб., 1861-1862

7. П.Е. Диакониссы первых веков христианства, Сергиев Посад. - 1909.

8. Добронравов Н., Диакониссы первых веков христианства, Сергиев Посад. - 1912.

9. Троицкий С., Диакониссы в Православной Церкви, - Спб., 1912

In addition, the following appeals, notes and reports to church hierarchy can be cited: "Explanotory Note on Aims and Goals of St. Martha and Mary Charity Abode Founded in Moscow" by great duchess St Elisabeth F. Romanov;[10] the "Report on Deaconesses to Holy Synod of Church of Russia" by Dmitrievsky[11] (both of these used the example of the St Martha and Mary sister community); the "Memorandum of the Lesna Female Monastery Rectress on the Foundation of the Deaconesses Community" by hiegumenia Ekaterina"[12] (who saw the deaconess order as a monastic one); "Rules of Deaconesses' Life and Activity" by Uspensky[13] (which were included by the IV department of the pre-consiliar bureau, chaired by Metropolitan Vladimir of Moscow, in 1906 on a project of parish statutes).

Metropolitan Vladimir of Moscow saw deaconesses as a parish-linked order, and not monastic; whereas the ideas of bishops on these issue were different. For example, Metropolitan Evlogy (Georgievsky) of Chelm thought that only the ministry should be revived, not the rank itself; while Stephan (Archangelsky) of Mogilev supported revival of the order. All the documents and statements on this issue as it was discussed in pre conciliar times and at the council itself are presented in "Discussions on the Question of Deaconesses at the Local Council of 1917-1918" by E. Beliacova and N. Beliakova[14]. According to this work, projects for decisions on the revival of the order of

10. Романова Е.Ф., вел. кн. Пояснительная записка о задачах и целях открывшейся в Москве Марфо-Мариинской обители милосердия.

11. Дмитриевский А.А., О диакониссах. Доклад Святейшему Синоду Русской Православной Церкви

12. Докладная записка настоятельницы Леснинского женского монастыря... об основании общины дьяконисс. 1905. РГИА, ф.796, оп. 445, д. 340, л.3.7., 4.

13. Успенский Ф., прот. Правила для жизни и деятельности православных диаконисс. - Журналы и протоколы и заседания Предсоборного Присутствия. Т. II . С. 102-104.

14. Белякова Е. В., Белякова Н. А., Обсуждение вопроса о диакониссах на Поместном Соборе 1917-1918 гг. // Церковно-исторический вестник, 2001. № 8. С. 139-161

deaconess were prepared, but formally decisions themselves were not taken (or, if they were, no documents remain), despite the important work done. The work of the council stopped as a result of the recurring repressions against the Orthodox Church in Soviet Russia, and for a long time, other issues became much more topical for church life.

The next wave of theoretical interest on the issue appeared in post-World War II era thanks to the works of Evangelos Theodorou in Greece. He was inspired by the example of Protestant deaconess sisterhoods and female diaconical activities of the Roman Catholic Church and published two works, *Heroines of Love: Deaconesses through the Ages*[15] (1949) and *The "Ordination" or "Appointment" of Deaconesses*[16] (1954). These works not only attempted to study the history of this order, but also investigated the liturgical sense of ordination to priestly ministry. His ideas were further developed in the 1988 Rhodes consultation document (1933-36)[17], and in *Women Deacons in the Orthodox Church: Called to Holiness and Ministry* by Kyriaky FirzGerald[18]. All the references in this paragraph were made in an ecumenical context, using examples of Protestant and Catholic studies, as well as with the support, and at the same time the challenges, of the ecumenical bodies – first and foremost, the World Council of Churches (WCC).

---

15. Θεοδώρου Ευ., *Ηρωίδες της χριστιανικής αγάπης – Αι διακόνισσαι δια των αιώνων*, Αθήναι, 1949.

16. Θεοδώρου Ευ., *Χειροτονία και χειροθεσία των Διακονισσών*, Αθήναι 1954.

17. "The Place of the Woman in the Orthodox Church and the Question of the Ordination of Women: Conclusions of an Inter-Orthodox Consultation—Rhodes, Greece, 30 October-7 November 1988", in Gennadios Limouris (ed.), *Orthodox Visions on Ecumenism: Statements, Messages and Reports on the Ecumenical Movement (1902-1992)*, WCC Publications, Geneva: 1997, p. 133-40.

18. K. FitzGerald, *Women Deacons in the Orthodox Church: Called to Holiness and Ministry*, Holy Cross Orthodox Press, Brookline, MA, 1988.

On the one hand, there are enough arguments of possibility and necessity for the restoration of the order of deaconesses. However if such ordinations were to happen[19], we have no reference to any ecclesial documents – in both the 19th and the 20th centuries and over the last decade such ordinations have been performed in unique situations and not established as a common church practice. First of all, they occur only in certain female monastic communities with a decision taken by the diocesial hierarch. No one can deny that according to tradition of the ancient Church (*argumentum ad traditio*), with reference to very prominent saint hierarchs (St Nektarios of Aegina, St Philaret of Moscow, St Nicolas of Japan, and other famous saints of our church (*argumentum ad verecundiam*)) with mention in the Bible, and with no theological obstacles, the order of deaconesses could be expected to flourish in the contemporary church.

But on the other hand, we cann't see the process of restoring this order. Even if we concede that ordination take place, such ordination is still ad hoc, occurring sporadically in very small numbers, not as a general rule but as exceptions. The female diaconate exists in the Bible, in history, in theology, and in practice as precedents, but it doesn't really exist in parish life. Even, to some extent, simply the good will of a bishop is needed for ordination (as it was in case of St Nectarios or St Philaret), but the majority do not have the courage to provide this.

That means that obstacles to the restoration of the order of deaconesses exist, and they are very strong. These obstacles are not of theological or traditional nature, they are rooted in something else – in an unwillingness of hierarchy, or in an unwillingness of church people, or in both. It is quite possible that we can find this in the

19. Sporadically some information on female ordination emerges in one or another local church, suggesting that some bishop ordained someone a deaconess or that there was some synodic decision on restoring the female diaconate; but normally it is impossible to find the source of such news, so I consider them hypothetical.

absence of church decision (which was not seen as an obstacle when discussed in Russia in the beginning of 20th century). As I see it, this is because females were excluded from priestly ministries for a long period of time in the Orthodox church, quite often connected with a fear of profanation of sacred things, and this fear doesn't allow us to cross the border psychologically.

Methodologically, this is quite the same thing as the discussion of married bishops in the Orthodox church or of married priests in the Roman Catholic church. This fear, the psychological rejection of phenomena, is quite irrational, even though quite often rational arguments are used for proving the existent (irrational) order of things: "It's better not to change something, even if it is very necessary and important, rather than to cause a schism". Orthodox quite often accuse "secularized" Protestants (i.e., in the issue of female ordination), arguing that the "female issue" is rooted not in the Church but in the secular feminist movement. But at the same time, many Orthodox people do not trust their hierarchy; and it seems the hierarchy feels this attitude too, so that the introduction of something in the Church that seems to be controversial is a threat as well. In some way this is a sign of the secularization of ecclesial consciousness, and from my point of view, apart from concrete issues in Church –like the female diaconate– this is a major, more general methodological issue that is always topical, and during preparatory time of the great and sacred council is more and more on agenda.

However, returning to the issue of female ordination as it exists in the Church today, in the ecumenical movement it becomes a less and less neutral issue. Orthodox often expressed their concern about female ordination in Protestant denominations, but at first this attitude was also opposed to the idea of female ordination being imposed on Orthodox during ecumenical encounters. But the order in certain communities was left upon themselves, as it was stated by Holy Synod of the Russian Orthodox Church in its statement on Fifth General Assembly of WCC and its implications: "We do not see any grounds against decisions on this topic in confessions, where priesthood is not recognized as sacrament, and, therefore from the point of view of orthodoxy, there is not at all sacramental priesthood as it is."[20].

Still, in ecumenical perspective this issue was raised by Orthodox as one of the tensions, but it never appeared to be a crucial one. To consider some examples,

- An appeal from an Orthodox participant to the WCC world conference on mission and evangelism (San-Antonio, 1989) stated that the "issue of more full participation of women in life of Church should become a subject of study in WCC, for us their ordination in holy rank is not a subject of discussion, because that contradicts Christology, ecclesiology, Tradition and practice of Ancient Church";[21]

- An appeal of Orthodox participants to the assembly of WCC (Canberra, 1991) stated that "the question of the ordination of women to the priestly and episcopal offices must also be understood within a theological and ecclesiological context[22];

- During the inter-Orthodox meeting in Chambesy (1991), the issue was not mentioned among challenges for Orthodox in the ecumenical movement, although it was underlined that this issue is a doctrinal one for Orthodox[23]. as well as naming female priesthood issue as an identity one for

20. Послание Священного Синода о V Ассамблее Всемирного Совета Церквей и ее результатах // Журнал Московской Патриархии. 1976, № 4. с. 9.
21. "Orthodox Letter to the WCC Conference on Mission and Evangelism—San-Antonio, USA, 31 May 1989", in Gennadios Limouris (ed.), *Orthodox Visions on Ecumenism*, p. 158.
22. "Reflections of Orthodox Participants Addressed to the Seventh Assembly of the World Council of Churches – Canberra, Australia, 7-20 February 1991," in Gennadios Limouris (ed.), *Orthodox Visions on Ecumenism*, p.177.
23. "The Orthodox Churches and the World Council of Churches: Report of an Inter-Orthodox Consultation of Orthodox WCC Member Churches – Chambesy, Switzerland, 12-16 September 1991", in Gennadios Limouris (ed.), *Orthodox Visions on Ecumenism*, p. 189-94.

Orthodox, which comes from the ecumenical movement and Orthodox are to protect themselves[24].

And there are other examples.

In the theological dialogue between the Russian Orthodox Church and Evangelischen Kirche in Deutschland, the election of female bishop Margot Kaessmann as a leader of EKD was crucial. It caused dramatic disputes, and even the cancellation of the celebration of the fifty-year jubilee of the theological dialogue. The Orthodox explanation was that "the situation has changed, as a woman has become the chairperson of the EKG. This raises a principal question of a prospect of maintaining dialogue in the mentioned form"[25]. Bishop Hilarion resorted to *argumentum ad populum*: "Besides, we cannot but take into account the opinion of our believers to whom meetings and talks with the church chaired by a woman are absolutely inadmissible"[26]. Patriarch Cyril of Moscow was even more strict,

> What has happened [the election of Kaessmann] has clearly revealed a fundamental difference between Orthodoxy and Protestantism and highlighted a major underlying problem: Orthodoxy safeguards the norm of apostolic faith and church order as sealed in the Holy Tradition of the Church and sees as its task to continually actualize this norm in carrying out its pastoral and missionary efforts[27].

24. Chambesy 1995 Metropolis Cyril of ROC "Orthodox vision of problems of modern ecumenism".
25. "Archbishop Hilarian's Letter to Chairperson of the Council of the Evangelical Church in Germany", *Russion Orthodox Church DECR*, 12 September 2009, at: http:// www. mospat.ru /en/2009/12/10/ news10042/
26. Ibid.
27. "Primate of the Russian Orthodox Church", *Russian Orthodox Church DECR*, 2 February 2010, at: http://www.mospat.ru/en/2010/02/02/news12456/

These examples are numerous, but even from these we can see how the "female" issue can become a crucial one in ecumenical relations, which not only makes it necessary for Orthodox to protect their position of not-ordaining females, it also complicates dialogue with non-Orthodox.

This need –to find arguments to protect and justify Orthodox practice– was a core motivation of the Agapia 1976 consultation. While recognizing the need to further study the office of female diaconate, the report of the consultation included the following statement,

> In light of the increasing debate on the ordination of women to the priesthood in churches of the Western tradition, it would be helpful to Orthodox women if special studies could be conducted on this subject in order to clarify and interpret the Orthodox position to other churches. This is an immediate need, especially for Orthodox women living in Western societies who are continually being engaged in dialogue on this questions[28].

Finding arguments always depends on motivation, and while one motivation was expressed as clarifying the Orthodox position to other churches, others can be to find arguments for supporting female priesthood or to make an attempt to dissociate from and impartially investigate the position.

This was the method of Elisabeth Behr-Sigel, whose fundamental theological research on the one hand inspired and on the other hand shocked many Orthodox theologians and believers. She presented quite strong arguments on the principal of the possibility of an ordained priesthood of women, and answered the main arguments against it: such as liturgical symbolism, the anthropological difference

---

28. "Orthodox Women: Their Role and Participation in the Orthodox Church: Report of an Inter-Orthodox Consultation – Agapia, Romania, 11-17 September 1976", in Gennadios Limouris (ed.), *Orthodox Visions on Ecumenism*, p. 60-65.

between men and women, Tradition, and others. Her weak points were that she was a convert from Protestantism and that she was a woman, so that many accusations *ad hominem* against her were made in this direction.

But the co-author of her book, *The Ordination of Women in the Orthodox Church*, Metropolitan Kallistos (Ware) of Diokleia, even if can be accused of being convert, cannot be accused of personal interest in introducing female priesthood into the Orthodox church. The book[29] remains the main reference for those who study, and even if it is not accepted institutionally, its theological courage has had a great impact on discussion of the issue. These two prominent theologians are not simply researchers looking for precedents. Their major thrust is that this is a methodological issue. It is not only a question of how concretely we can interpret a certain issue or phenomenon in Scripture, Tradition, dogma, or Church life, but also a question of how we can interpret and study Scripture, Tradition, dogma, and Church life. Which argument is enough? Which argument can be considered and which cannot? These questions are very important ones, and discussing ordination of women as priests, not merely deaconesses, can give us many methodological answers also in theology.

The arguments used on the issue of female ordination to priesthood are many. The main inter-Orthodox document was adopted more than thirty years ago at the Rhodes consultation: *The Place of the Woman in the Orthodox Church and the Question of the Ordination of Women*[30]. The document, affirming anthological equality of men and women and royal priesthood of all the faithful despite their sex,

---

29. Elisabeth Behr-Sigel & Kallistos Ware, *The Ordination of Women in the Orthodox Church*, WCC Publications, Geneva, 2000.
30. "The Place of the Woman in the Orthodox Church and the Question of the Ordination of Women: Conclusions of an Inter-Orthodox Consultation – Rhodes, Greece, 30 October-7 November 1988", in Gennadios Limouris (ed.), *Orthodox Visions on Ecumenism*, p. 133-40

outlines the following position, rooted in the sacramental character of the Church, on why women are excluded from sacerdotal or special priesthood,

- the Lord did not choose a woman for apostolic mission;
- Theotokos provides women with a model and she was not ordained as a priest;
- it is against apostolic tradition and practice;
- Pauline teachings.

The most interesting idea in the document was the proposal of the typological approach to human sexual belonging – "Adam-Christ" for male, and "Eve-Mary" (and also church) for female. This typology determines the special content of the ministry of woman in the work of the recapitulation of New Adam, through the creative descent of the Holy Spirit, as it happened with the Virgin Mary, Theotokos. Of course, this typology can be only symbolical – all people, both men and women, are saved by Christ and through Christ, and our relationship with Christ is also equal for men and women. The proposed typology is only symbolic, not connected directly to the difference between the sexes.

The authors of the document mention that "this typological relationship provides the foundation of the general content of the consciousness of the church concerning the impossibility of ordaining women to the Christocentric sacramental Priesthood". This typology balances Christology and Pneumatology in the Church. The analogical, typological, symbolical approach is not a dogmatic approach. As we can see, when it comes to dogmatics, the authors encounter a problem with the explanation, so they state, "The manner in which we approach God and the way we understand women and men is not left solely to our limited reason, valuable though it is",

> ...We are not simply dealing with theological concepts and ideas. We are in a sphere of profound, almost indescribable

experience of the inner ethos of the world-saving and cosmic dimensions of Christ truth. The iconic and typological mode of dealing with the issue tells us that rational constructs will not be adequate alone to describe and express it fully. Like all of the mysteries of the Faith as lived in Orthodoxy, this one too is articulated with the fear of God and with a sense of reverence... We sense that our words are words of truth and not mere apologetics.

As we can see, rational arguments, theological concepts and ideas cannot explain church practice, but "almost indescribable experience" is called an argumentation. In theological discussion, this can be very destructive. If we take a typological approach as a dogmatic one, we can assert –and many people do– that men have a special relationship with Christ while women a have special relationship with Theotokos. Here, we are mixing visual likeness with anthological likeness. The difference between Christ (as not only man but Son of God, as the second person of the Holy Trinity who accepted human nature but not additional human personality) and us (both men and women) is much more crucial than that between Christ and Theotokos, who is a human being in her personality.

This again raises a methodological issue – can such a typological and sometimes poetic approach be used in theological discussion as a foundation for conclusions? If we say "Eve is from Adam, that's why she is subordinate to him", can't we use it as an analogy for saying "Jesus was born from Mary, that's why Second Person of the Holy Trinity is subordinate to women" (or some such argument).

Taking the typological or analogical approach to this issue is not an unusual occurrence. Further examples of such argumentation can be mentioned here.

Shmaliy in his paper at the Russian Orthodox Church conference on anthropology examines the issue of differences between the sexes in human nature through an anthropological perspective. Asserting sexual duality, he argues that sexes exist in a hierarchical relationship because male is arche, the beginning of female, due to the fact that Eve is from Adam and not vice versa. Shmaliy extends the analogical approach even further, comparing the relationship between Adam and Eve to the relationship among the Holy Trinity, where Adam corresponds to the Holy Father, and Eve to Logos,

> Monarchism of Father in the Most Holy Trinity doesn't belittle consubstantiality of Son and Holy Spirit, in the same way monarchism of man doesn't belittle dignity of woman. But it could be crazy to imagine the intention of Son to het power of Father, so it is strange to claim that woman become equal to man in all. Difference in the service of man and woman in Church is related with this hierarchy[31].

Balashov, referring to works of Behr-Sigel and Ware, notes that the theological foundations of the opponents of female priesthood are quite weak, insisting that motivation for discussing female priesthood "is not of Christ, but of the elements of this world"[32], and that this is enough to ignore the argumentation. He sees that sexes have different functions, and one of the main functions of women is motherhood. The social role of the female should be first of all in correspondence with this fundamental devotion of woman as wife and mother.

A special report on female priesthood was made at the Russian Orthodox Church conference on sacramentology by Posternak[33].

---

31. Шмалий В., свящ. Проблематика пола в свете христианской антропологии (Быт 1. 27) // Богословская конференция Русской Православной Церкви «Учение Церкви о человеке». Москва, 5–8 ноября 2001 г. Материалы. М., 2002. С. 281–320.

32. Балашов Н., прот. Актуальные вопросы этики пола в свете «Основ социальной концепции Русской Православной Церкви» // Богословская конференция Русской Православной Церкви «Учение Церкви о человеке». Москва, 5–8 ноября 2001 г. Материалы. М., 2002. С. 321–332.

33. Постернак А., свящ. Вопрос о «женском священстве». Доклад на Богословской Конференции Русской Православной Церкви «Православное

He mentions not just two problems – the status of woman in relation to man according to Christian anthropology and the elusiveness of priesthood ministry – but also a third, methodological one – the possibility of evolution and transformation of Tradition. On the anthropological level, he repeats that there is sexual differentiation as well as a hierarchy of sexes (albeit with ontological equality) that can be found in the relationship of Adam and Eve. Woman is subordinate to man, and giving birth is the main condition for her salvation. As a testimony to this hierarchy, institutional priesthood has a male character. Symbolism and iconic character of priesthood, typological approach - the argument used in Rodos document - is considered as sophism, as well as issue of the accessibility of priesthood, while only hierarchy of sexes can be enough as an argument for the elusiveness.

Speaking of the evolution of Tradition, Posternak refers to the fact that many ministries in the Church, such as deaconesses, disappeared, while other institutionalized female ministries (elders, widows and virgins) were transformed into nuns. All attempts to revive the order of female diaconate were unsuccessful, and this is evidence of Tradition as alive and changing – old and untimely forms of ministries transform and disappear. On the other hand, he does not explain the mechanisms of these processes and denounces those who proclaim the need for church Tradition to be revised.

Posternak, like his predecessors, adds further arguments,
- that the issue of female priesthood is rooted not in Scripture of church Tradition, but in Western feminism;
- that revision of tradition can lead also to revision of Scripture;
- that the destruction of the hierarchy of sexes and their natural functions led to the catastrophe of the institution of family.

учение о церковных таинствах», Москва, 13-16 ноября 2007 г., секция «Таинство священства»: http://theolcom.ru/ru/full_text.php

Taking in consideration all these problems he comes to conclusion that the issue of female priesthood is not a question for the Orthodox church; it is a question that is destructive in nature.

From my point of view, this issue, which seems to be theoretical, creates a challenging and creative situation, in which all methodological issues can be touched upon. It also moved theologians to see the issue of gender in an anthropological framework, to discuss the issues of nature and personality and of the church and its ministries on new levels. For me, this is big issue: why in the Russian empire at the beginning of 20th century was the restoration of female diaconal order so close, when now, after women have established a much more equal place in society through the feminist movement, this issue is much further away from being resolved? Does it mean that different types of argumentation had different meaning and impact on theological discussions and ecclesial decisions? Does it mean that prominent hierachs of those times were more courageous? Does it mean that people in the Church were more ready for reforms in Church order and hierarchy and had more trust? Are we really looking for truth and authenticity in theological reflections or are we just trying to find and protect our identity?

Kuraev[34], arguing against woman as priests, enumerates many exclusively female characteristics: women are paradoxical, exhibit hysterical religiosity (which is why, according to Kuraev, the apostle Paul forbad them to speak in church), and are rigorous, instructive and sensitive (he illustrates this final quality with a scenario of confession, when the face of a sensitive woman priest might reflect the sins of the confessing person, making confession uncomfortable). Don't we too often in theology follow psychological arguments? Or too seldom explore our own psychology to find that many theological ideas have

---

34. Кураев А., диак. Церковь в мире людей. Женщина в Церкви. - http://www.pravoslavie.ru/put/6031.htm.

roots not in theology itself, not in Scripture, not in Tradition, but in some constructs of our unconscious – not in rational arguments, but in irrational fears?

I think Orthodox have been too concentrated on human nature, sacrificing the notion of human personality; on ideas, and not on its perception; on Tradition as something in the past rather than something now and for the future. Which is more authentic? The Tradition we are used to? I don't know how to answer these questions. And I am not ready to start with the answers immediately. I already have too many answers, too many arguments that seem to be equally correct and reasonable. We, Orthodox in the ecumenical movement, declare quite often that our vocation is to provide answers on Orthodoxy, but I think it is also good to formulate questions – to others and to ourselves.

UNITY IN SUFFERING AND HOPE: A REFLECTION ON ORTHODOX WOMEN'S PARTICIPATION IN THE ECUMENICAL MOVEMENT

AIKATERINI PEKRIDOU

"Life is unfair. Who told you it is fair?"
"I'm fine. Haven't found a job yet, still trying…"
"Research is going well, but I find this life a bit difficult…"
"I don't know why, these days I'm feeling immensely depressed."
"Anyway, life seems to be hell here… planning to move but it's tough."
"Remember that Christ is there to help you."
"You and your family were much in thought and prayer today."
"We managed to worship in the church today. God is gracious!"
"I trust that God will open doors that we might not even be aware of right now."
"It is not possible to live between two worlds. I choose the Light, I choose Christ!"

These are text messages that I received from friends around the world during the last year. Messages from incredible women and men committed to Church and Christian unity which reveal the difficulties, the reality of pain and suffering they experience in their lives, but also the hopes and joys of their life in Christ.

In the ecumenical movement, we often talk about the differences among churches in doctrinal and ethical teaching, church structures, administration of sacraments, liturgical order or types of services, or the different understandings of mission and service of the church in the world. Important as this aspect of dialogue is, so that one day Christians receive together the body and blood of Christ and witness to the world their communion with God and creation[1], our com-

---

1. It is important to be reminded of the Commission on Faith and Order's by-laws:

monality of being affected in the same way by sin, suffering and pain should not be neglected, and our faith in Christ as our Saviour and hope must not be overlooked[2].

Orthodox women, like all men and women in the world, regardless of age, cultural background, social, educational and economic status, are confronted with the reality of suffering and failure. As humans we are all united in our anxiety for the future. The fear of pain, and ultimately death, is a challenge to us all. And this is a story as old as the human race.

However, as Christians we live in the conviction that the kingdom of God will put an end to all the suffering we experience as created human beings. We lay our hopes to Christ and seek the overcoming of all pain, hostility and division (Rom. 5:1-11). In we yearn for reconciliation with one another, with our creator and nature (Col. 1:19-20). And all this in a world that carries the burdens and heritage of its past, but also brings new perspectives and elements.

ANXIETIES AND NEEDS OF THE YOUNGER GENERATION

What is becoming an anxiety of every day life for the younger generation is the need for meaningful education, one that would desirably result in securing a reasonably paid job linked to the fulfillment of basic human needs and possibly a respectable social status. As higher education is becoming a luxury (due to increases of fees of higher

"to proclaim the oneness of the Church of Jesus Christ and to call the churches to the goal of visible unity in one faith and one eucharistic fellowship expressed in worship and in common life in Christ, in order that the world may believe", in Thomas F. Best (ed.), *Faith and Order at the Crossroads: The Plenary Commission Meeting, Kuala Lumpur 2004*, Faith and Order Paper No. 196, WCC, Geneva, 2005, p. 450.

2. See His Beatitude Archbishop Anastasios of Tirana and All Albania, "Message from the 13th General Assembly of CEC to All the Member Churches and Called to One Hope in Christ, Sermon for the Gathering Service", CEC at: "http://assembly.ceceurope.org/index.

institutions, and financial difficulties and budget cuts taking place in institutions worldwide) and while unemployment continuously threatens the younger generations, education and work have turned into a constant source of anxiety and uncertainty rather than serving as the foundation for the creative use of new ideas, talents, imagination and energy.

Furthermore, migration, another distinctive phenomenon of our time –whether voluntary or forced for educational, economic, political or environmental reasons– affects mostly younger people. As recent statistics show, migration affects especially women, to the extent that we talk today about the "feminization of migration"[3]. Western societies have come to realize that they are not only receiving people, but also sending their own people away in the hope of a life of dignity and comfort. Whether migrants succeed in earning respect and the fulfillment of their hopes in their new countries and in the context of the local established churches is another painful story[4].

Related to the struggle for a better future and the changes that migration brings to social and family life is one more anxiety: that of young people to create and sustain a family. Again, women are severely affected. That is not to say that men face fewer difficulties, but there are factors that put extra pressure on women, such as the still existing silent "demand" of traditional societies for women to raise children in order to fulfill their purpose of existence in the world, and also the biological limitations of age.

---

3. For migration in Europe see the WCC-commissioned study Darrell Jackson & Alessia Passarelli, *Mapping Migration: Mapping Churches' Responses, Europe Study*, CCME & Nova Research Center, 2008. For migration on the global level and the work of the Global Ecumenical Network on Migration see: http://www.oikoumene. org/en/news/newsonselectedcategory.html.
4. It is shocking how relevant the words of migrant women in the 1978 edition of the book *Migrant Women Speak* are still today. This book was published for the then Churches Committee on Migrant Workers, Search Press Limited, London/WCC, Geneva.

With regard to this fluid social framework, and the challenges to the younger generation and especially women, there is an imperative for churches to be able to read the world to which they are called to bring the Good News of salvation. To this end, theological education becomes of particular importance, especially as young generations realize the need for theological studies to engage with the contemporary concerns and achievements of other scientific areas. A need is underlined for theology to be aware of and in dialogue with the contributions of other disciplines, which results in a deepened understanding of the complexity of the world where the Gospel is incarnate.

At the same time, looking at the life of our Christian communities and their decision-making bodies, one understands the still weak participation of women in them. As the ecumenical movement reflects the reality of our churches, the same applies to the representation of our churches in the instruments of the ecumenical movement. One can agree that after decades of ecumenical endeavours, there is still need to create space for a women's full participation in the life of the Church and the ecumenical movement. There is still need for brothers and sisters, branches of the same vine, to ensure that the gifts of women will grow and flourish in the life of the Church and also in the context of the ecumenical dialogue.

Moreover, there is an increasing awareness among the younger generation of theologians and committed Christians (who do not necessarily hold degrees in theology) of the need to really know the partners involved in the ecumenical dialogue; to actually engage in their lives, in their sufferings and joys. The mobility of young people contributes to a growing desire to encounter the Christian traditions and living faiths by experiencing the agonies and hopes of the faith communities as they really are at present, and not as described in dated manuals of theology. At the same time, there is an increasing awareness that Christians are not the only created images of God in this world; and definitely they are not the only ones who believe they possess the Truth, who believe in a Divine Entity, a God to whom they lay all their hopes.

This realization opens up a whole new perspective to churches on how to live and articulate their faith in the world. It provides them with new insights on how they define their identity as the Body of Christ in the presence of "the other". It challenges the understanding of being Church of the established churches and questions the way they define their existence and mission in the world. While more and more Christians affirm their faith in Christ, but deny being identified with any particular tradition, and as "the other", who lives now in our neighborhood and parish and has his/her own perception of what it means to be Church, there is an urgency for an intentional and more systematic study of other Christian traditions, inter-Christian relations and inter-religious dialogue.

Because the social and ecclesial landscape changes so rapidly, it is also of vital importance to be aware of the position and roles of women in the different faith communities and to ensure their voices are heard in the ecumenical debate. As Orthodox women faithfully engaged in dialogue, we are committed on the one hand to witness our Christian faith, and on the other hand to ensure that those women who are less heard (e.g., migrant, indigenous, youth) have the opportunity to express themselves freely in an environment of mutual respect. We have to create such conditions so that they are able to speak of themselves in order that the ecumenical encounter bears fruit.

These ideas might not be totally new. In fact, older generations of theologians, from different standpoints perhaps, addressed many of the issues mentioned here. However, what is new in the present moment is the realization of the failure of political and economic systems worldwide to give people hope for the future and a sense of security. Men and women in the Global South as much as in the Global North, experience the limitations of political, economic and social systems to bring about a just and peaceful world; they are confronted with the pain deriving from the world's systems being unsuccessful to give human life meaning.

At the same time, a distinctive mark of our time –whether characterized as post modernity, late modernity, or new modernity– is an increasing feeling of dissatisfaction among young people combined with an attitude of challenging the traditional values of churches and sources of authority, as well as questioning any kind of hierarchy in the life of the churches. There is an "I've had enough" feeling of young people towards society and the institutional Church, whose possible consequences, I am afraid, are not sensed by the majority of our churches. There is an underlying anger against any source of power along with the feeling that no supreme authority can indicate to believers how to live their lives in relation to God, or convince them in matters of faith, unless the responses to the questions posed by engagement in society satisfy the hearts and minds of the faithful.

THE WAY FORWARD

In this perspective, the Volos meeting of 2008 on Orthodox women's participation in the ecumenical movement, and the subsequent publication itself, become of particular importance, as a witness of faith of Orthodox women in today's world. They signify the renewal of Orthodox women's commitment to the ecumenical movement. With the support and sponsorship of the programme for Women in Church and Society of the World Council of Churches (WCC), the meeting brought together concerns and perspectives of women involved for decades in the ecumenical movement who worked for an active liturgical, diaconal and administrative participation of women in the church, as well as the concerns and insights of the younger generation, evaluating Orthodox women's status in the church and the ecumenical organizations.

From exploring the past theological and ecumenical concerns of Orthodox women and assessing the current ones, participants dove into the theological issues and challenges on women's participation and ministry in the Church, as well as the ambivalences of the role of Orthodox women in the church. They examined the essential elements of theology discussing it in conjunction with ecclesial praxis and women's involvement in Christian and inter-religious dialogue. To that end, ecumenical contributions of particular women were elevated as examples for future work, and the experiences were shared of Orthodox women involved in ecumenical work in local communities around the world.

During the small group discussions, it became evident that there are still issues with which Orthodox women are concerned and which have not been addressed adequately so far. Therefore, some concrete proposals were put forward[5], such as the need to affirm women's dignity through a deeper understanding of their biology (with regard to the prayers and practices associated with women's menstrual cycle); and the need for sponsorship of Orthodox women to pursue studies in theology and for support so as to be employed within the Church. Further, an active involvement of Orthodox women was emphasized with regard to pastoral and diaconal work, the minor orders and newer ministries that are connected to the liturgical life of the community, as well as with regard to decision-making bodies.

In addition to a creative use of Orthodox women's skills and strengthening their contributions in the leadership of the Church and ecumenical organizations, I believe there is a vital role that Orthodox women can play in the process of ecumenical reception. As they are increasingly engaged in education and hold teaching positions at all levels, they are given a unique opportunity to discuss the agreements reached on the ecumenical level and make the decisions known to their community – whether that is the class, their parish or the broader academic community. Orthodox women hold positions that allow

5. See "Report of the Inter-Orthodox Consultation, 'And many women were there…' (Matt. 27:55): Participation of Orthodox Women in the Ecumenical Movement: Past, Present, Future, Volos, Greece, 8-12 June 2008", WCC website: http://www.oikoumene.org/en/resources/documents/wccprogrammes/ecumenicalmovement-in-the-21st-century/women/participation-of-orthodox-women-in-the-ecumenicalmovement.htm.

them to introduce new people in the ecumenical concerns and debate, to share the resources that are available and prepare the way for meaningful reflection and action on the decisions reached by churches.

Christian women, like the woman in the gospel according to Luke who suffered for eighteen long years (Luke 13:10-17), do not give up hope, endure and continue to pray to God despite the suffering and pain they experience in life. Through their remarkable ability to create strong bonds of friendship and network, today's women, like those other women (Matt. 28:1-10) who were the first to meet the resurrected Christ, are called together with men to witness Christ as the hope in a world that is suffering and a life that is wounded. In Him we cannot despair because we live in the conviction that He is with us "always, to the end of the age" (Matt. 28:20).

WOMEN IN INTER-RELIGIOUS DIALOGUE WITHIN THE WCC AND ORTHODOX CHRISTIANITY'S INITIATIVES

Aggeliki Ziaka

> *"In our encounter with the other*
> *we learn about ourselves...*
> *how to understand ourselves (as Christians)*
> *within the religious diversity of the world."*
> Hans Ucko, Témoignage, Pro Dialogo 1994

The term dialogue (from the Greek verb *dialegomai*) signifies an interaction; a conversation between two or more parties who exchange opinions and ideas and, in negotiating a problem, create consensus and bridge opposing views. Therefore, moderation is a constitutive element of dialogue, which makes it possible to solve problems through constructive and honest dialogue: "not quarrelling but conversing dialogically" is the formulation of the pre-eminently dialectical philosopher, Plato[1]. It is a living and vibrant discourse that wells up in the souls of conversants. The interplay of question and answer ignites in the soul the spark which, after a prolonged period of common pursuits and dialogical efforts, flashes in the recesses of the soul and offers illumination. Therefore, dialogue is not an art pertaining to pugnacious disputants, a form of contest that privileges attempts to impose one's opinions through well aimed questions and answers bound to cause tensions and dissent. Rather, it is the art of establishing equal terms in the endeavours of those in converse to make a spiritual turn and begin the quest for knowledge in search of the truth, transcending the epistemological realm marked by the *aporia* of ignorance.

Throughout the history of religions, dialogue has focused on issues of faith, worship and social and moral life. Informal, incomplete and unrecorded attempts at dialogue on these issues must, no doubt,

---

1. *Republic* 454A, see also 511C, *Theaet.* 167E ff.

date to a very early age, or at least to the first encounters of dissimilar, diverging or even opposing systems of faith. The term "inter-religious dialogue" was widely disseminated in various religious traditions and became fairly common, especially after the first world war. Inter-religious dialogues and the study of world religions are conducive to promoting understanding and communication between nations with different religious faiths, social life and culture. Hence, inter-religious dialogues are also frequently termed "intercultural". Inter-religious and intercultural dialogue affords the participants the opportunity to appreciate the cultural and religious values of different traditions, making the world more friendly and familiar. Today, inter-religious dialogue is promoted by the Orthodox, Catholic and Protestant churches. The removal of the opposing grounds of "I" and "You" and our acquaintance with and respect for other traditions are the most fruitful and realistic means of ensuring the peaceful co-existence of nations and forestalling religious conflict.

INTER-RELIGIOUS DIALOGUE AND ORTHODOXY

The inter-religious dialogue of the Orthodox Church is based on two encyclicals of the Orthodox patriarchate of Constantinople: (i) the 1902 encyclical addressed to the metropolitan, bishops and bishops under the canonical jurisdiction of the Ecumenical Patriarchate, in which Patriarch Joachim III exhorted them to intensify their efforts to initiate a dialogue, strengthen interconfessional rapport and re-inforce the unity of the Orthodox churches, and (ii) the 1920 encyclical, a document of historical importance, which for the first time articulated the proposal of the Ecumenical Patriarchate to create a "Society of Churches" based on the Society of Nations which had been founded immediately after the end of first world war (Versailles, 18.1.1919). These encyclicals should be numbered amongst the most significant texts of the ecumenical movement. They led to a regular rapport between Orthodox, Catholic and ancient Eastern churches and the establishment of the two well-known branches of the ecumenical movement: Life and Work (Stockholm 13-30.8.1925) and Faith and Order (Lausanne 3-21.8.1927). The merging of these two branches, just after the climactic events of the second world war, would eventually lead to the founding of the World Council of Churches (WCC) in Amsterdam in September 1948, on which most Orthodox churches are represented under the banner of the Patriarchate of Constantinople[2].

The WCC would express a deep interest not only in the unity of the Christian churches, but also in the establishment of an inter-religious dialogue with a view to achieving global unity. The third general meeting of the WCC in New Delhi (1961) gave new impetus to the notion of a dialogue with other religions, though the steps taken at that time were fraught with grave reservations[3]. In the WCC, inter-

2. G. Tsetsis, *The Contribution of The Ecumenical Patriarchate to the Establishment of the World Council of Churches (Η συμβολή του οικουμενικού Πατριαρχείου στην ίδρυση του Παγκοσμίου Συμβουλίου Εκκλησιών)*, Tertios, Katerini, 1986. See also C. G. Patelos (ed.), *The Orthodox Church in the Ecumenical Movement (Documents and Statements 1902-1975)*, WCC Publications, Geneva, 1978; N. Matsoukas, *Ecumenical Movement, History—Theology (Οικουμενική κίνηση, ιστορία-θεολογία)*, Pournaras, Thessaloniki, 1986, p. 214-27. St. Tsompanidis, an assistant professor in the University of Thessaloniki's Department of Theology, has written an exhaustive series of studies on the Orthodox Church, the ecumenical dialogue, and the WCC entitled "The Orthodox Church and the World Council of Churches: A 'Community' of Mutual Enrichment on the Path of Inquiry" («*Η Ορθόδοξη Εκκλησία και το Παγκόσμιο Συμβούλιο των Εκκλησιών. Μια «κοινωνία» αμοιβαίου εμπλουτισμού στο δρόμο των αναζητήσεων*»), *History of Orthodoxy, Volume 8: Orthodoxy in Dialogue*, Road, Athens, p. 224-369; Idem, *The Contribution of the Orthodox Church and Theology to the World Council of Churches: In Favor of the Union of All (Η Συμβολή της Ορθόδοξης Εκκλησίας και Θεολογίας στο Παγκόσμιο Συμβούλιο των Εκκλησιών. Υπέρ της των πάντων ενώσεως)*, Pournaras, Thessaloniki, 2008; Idem, *Orthodoxie und Okumene. Gemeinsam auf dem Weg su Gerechtigkeit, Frieden und Bewahrung der Schopfung.* Mit einem Vorwort von Ulrich Duchrow (Ökumenische Studien 10), Lit Verlag, Münster, Hamburg, London, 1999.

3. *The New Delhi Report: The Third Assembly of the WCC,* London, SCM, 1961.

religious dialogue assumed an institutional form when the department for Dialogue with People of Living Faiths and Ideologies was established in the 1970s[4]. From the first moment, this institutional initiative was embraced by the Orthodox, who also developed a strong interest in Christian-Islamic dialogue in the context of the Conference of European Churches (CEC).

It should be clear that the Orthodox Church was an active catalyst in the rapid developments during the first decades of the 20th century that would culminate in the two great world wars. The Orthodox Church proposed initiatives and actions crucial to the unity not only of the Christian churches but of the world as a whole. The patriarchal encyclicals referred to above voice the concern of the mother church in the face of the fragmentation of church and world[5].

The most important step toward the opening of the Ecumenical Patriarchate to other religions was taken in 1961 at the First Panorthodox Conference in Rhodes, where the issue of "Orthodoxy and other Religions" was included on the agenda for the preparation of the eighth ecumenical synod, which is yet to be convened[6]. A specific and express decision to initiate a pan orthodox dialogue with other religions was taken at the First Prosynodic Panorthodox Conference at the Ecumenical Patriarchate Orthodox Centre in Chambésy. For the Orthodox Church expressed the will to contribute to inter-religious understanding and hence to endeavours to eradicate

---

4. *Guidelines on Dialogue with People of Living Faiths and Ideologies*, Geneva, WCC, 1979.

5. V. Stavridis, *History of Ecumenical Mouvement (Ἰστορία Οἰκουμενικῆς Κοινήσεως-ΑΒ47α)*, Πατριαρχικό Ἴδρυμα Πατερικῶν Μελετῶν, Μονή Βλατάδων, Thessaloniki, 1984 & 1996. Idem, *History of the Ecumenical Patriarchate (1453-Present) (Ἰστορία τοῦ Οἰκουμενικοῦ Πατριαχείου)*, Kyriakides & Kyriakides, Thessaloniki, 1987, 1999, p. 51-57, 248, 321- 36 (in Greek).

6. G. Martzelos, "Orthodoxy and Interreligious Dialogue" (Ὀρθοδοξία καὶ Διαθρησκειακός Διάλογος), *Ecclesia-Oekumene-Policy*. A Volume Presented to the Metropolitan Bishop of Adrianople Damaskinos. Interparliamentary Assembly on Orthodoxy, Athens, 2007: 437-44, esp. p. 440.

fanaticism on all sides, so that the ideals of liberty and peace might prevail in the world to the benefit of every human being irrespective of race or religion. This proposal was renewed and further elaborated in the Third Prosynodic Panorthodox Conference, convened in 1986 in the Ecumenical Patriarchate Orthodox Centre in Chambésy, which determined the principles that were to govern the contribution of the Orthodox Church to the spread of the spirit of peace, justice, liberty, fraternity and charity among nations and religious traditions and to the elimination of racial prejudice, or indeed any kind of prejudice[7].

Currently, inter-religious dialogue is being promoted by Ecumenical Patriarch Bartholomew I, who in his inaugural message following his enthronement on 2 November 1991 stressed both the importance of the unity of the Orthodox faith and the exalted duty of the Church to humankind. For the Ecumenical Patriarchate, this duty consists in sustaining a dialogue with the other great world religions and in preserving the universal spiritual and moral heritage that crowns our humanity. Thus, the Ecumenical Patriarchate regards inter-religious dialogue as both necessary and essential. Standing firmly on the established traditions of the past, the Ecumenical Patriarchate offers itself and its centuries-old knowledge concerning issues of co-existence with a view to a renewed and modern dialogue with the other world religions, especially the monotheistic religions of Judaism and Islam.

Dialogues with Judaism were initiated in 1977 and dialogues with Islam followed in 1986[8]. One of the architects of the inter-religious

---

7. Damaskinos Papandreou, "Pan-orthodox Conferences", *The Encyclopedia of Christianity*, Volume 4, Eerdamns/Brill, 2005, p. 25-26.

8. J. Karavidopoulos, "Dialogue between Orthodoxy and Judaism", *Global Meeting for Religion and Cultures*, Proceedings of a Conference for Peace (in Greek), Kykkos Monastery, Cyprus, 2002, p. 181-84; Gr. Ziakas, "The Dialogues of the Patriarchate of Constantinople with Islam" (in Greek), *Phanari: 400 Years*, Publications of the Orthodox Patriarchate, 2001, p. 575-725. Idem, "Living in Harmony with People of Other Faiths" (Θρησκειολογικά Μελετήματα. Τόμος Α: Ζώντας αρμονικά με ανθρώπους διαφορετικής σκέψης) (in Greek), in P. Pachis (ed. Shmaliy), *Studies on Religion. Volume I*, Vanias, Thessaloniki, 2004.

dialogues with Judaism and Islam, Damaskinos Papandreou, then-Metropolitan Bishop of Switzerland (now Metropolitan Bishop of Adrianople), offers a fine starting point for our understanding of the state of affairs,

> The initiatives undertaken by the Orthodox Centre of the Ecumenical Patriarchate to organise academic meetings with representatives of Judaism as well as Islam articulate the broader intention of the Ecumenical Patriarchate to render a positive contribution to ensuring the peaceful co-existence of the faithful of the three monotheistic religions, who inhabit the same geographical space and face common problems[9].

To aid the proper conduct and minister to these dialogues, the Ecumenical Patriarchate set up a Committee on the Dialogue with Islam in 1973, in the years of Patriarch Demetrius I. Nevertheless, it was the Centre of the Ecumenical Patriarchate at Chambésy (Geneva) that became the focus of inter-Orthodox, inter-confessional and inter-religious dialogues. The Centre was founded following a decision by the Ecumenical Patriarch Athenagoras and the Holy Synod jointly taken in 1966. The Co-ordinating Committee for the Promotion of Dialogue between Christians and Muslims, similar to the Islam committee on dialogue, was set up at the Centre in 1966. In the same Orthodox Centre in Chambésy, the Centre for Inter-religious and Inter-cultural Research and Dialogue was founded, with headquarters in Geneva and offices in Houston (USA) and Amman (Jordan), following an initiative by His Grace Damaskinos, then-Metropolitan Bishop of Switzerland, and with the blessings of the Ecumenical Patriarch.

---

9. Bishop of Switzerland Damaskinos Papandreou, "The Interreligious Dialogue of the Orthodox Church" ("Οι διαθρησκειακοί διάλογοι της ορθοδόξου Εκκλησίας") (in Greek), in M. Constantinou & Alfred Stirnemann (eds.), *The Dialogue between Christianity and Islam as a Common Duty: Dialogue and Speculation* 2. Society for Ecumenical Studies (Thessaloniki) and the Pro Oriente Institute (Vienna), Paratiritis, Thessaloniki, 1998, p. 31-51, esp. p. 33.

This centre has now been incorporated into the Brussels Office of the Ecumenical Patriarchate in the European Union. This foundation was set up with broader horizons and the mission to enable dialogue between both the monotheistic and other major world religions. A new institute (foundation) for Inter-religious and Intercultural Research and Dialogue was established in Geneva, Switzerland, in May 1999. Its aspiration is to create a foundation that will support the Center of Inter-religious and Intercultural Research and Dialogue[10]. The European Union office of the Ecumenical Patriarchate and the Vlatades Initiative represent important steps towards promoting panorthodox, inter-denominational and inter-religious relations[11].

The official publication of the Ecumenical Patriarchate, *Theologia*, registers the numerous and diverse actions and activities of the Ecumenical Patriarchate, which are intended to ensure the orderly functioning of the mother Church, her rapport with other Orthodox churches and Christian denominations and to promote her diverse relations and dialogue with the world and different religious traditions for the sake of spreading peace and justice amongst humankind. Accounts of activities pertaining to pan orthodox and interdenominational relations as well as inter-religious dialogues under the auspices of the Ecumenical Patriarchate Orthodox Centre in Chambésy appear in the *Episkepsis* review, the Centre's official publication.

10. The Foundation is honoured that Pope Benedict XVI, a co-founder and former board of trustees member, graciously accepts this presentation and so underlines his continued commitment to a common vision of promoting understanding, tolerance and friendship among the three monotheistic religions: Judaism, Christianity, and Islam. Retrieved from http://popespeaks.wordpress.com/2007/02/12/address-to-the-foundation-for-inter-religious-and-intercultural-research-and-dialogue-1-february-2007.
See G. Papademetriou, "Establishment of the Institute for Inter-religious and Intercultural Research and Dialogue", *Journal of Ecumenical Studies* 39.1-2 (Winter-Spring 2002), p. 399.
11. A. Ziaka, "Interreligious Dialogue", *History of Orthodoxy, Volume 8: Orthodoxy in Dialogue*, Road, Athens, p. 532-67, esp. 532-55.

There is no doubt that inter-religious dialogue is also promoted by other Orthodox churches: the Patriarchate of Alexandria, which seeks to advance its relations with Islam as well as traditional religions of African countries within the area of its canonical jurisdiction; the Patriarchate of Antioch, where the dialogue with and the research on Islam have benefited from the insights of George Khodre, Bishop of Lebanon[12] while religious studies are continually advanced by the University of Balamand's St. John Damascene School of Theology; the Russian Church, headed by its Patriarchate, which has established relations not only with Muslims but also with Buddhists and the sundry religious traditions in the vast area inhabited by Christians under its jurisdiction. Further information on the activities of other Orthodox patriarchates and autocephalous churches[13] could be added here, but lack of space imposes limitations on furnishing more details.

INTER-RELIGIOUS DIALOGUE AND WOMEN

More and more women scholars and politicians have participated in inter-religious conferences and meetings in recent decades, especially from 1990 onward. However, the participation of women remains

12. Georgios Khodr, Metropolitan Bishop of Mt. Lebanon, "Koinonia in Witness", in Thomas Best and Gunther Gassman (eds.), *On the Way to Fuller Koinonia: Official Report of the Fifth World Conference on Faith and Order, Santiago de Compostella, 1993*, Faith and Order Paper No. 166, WCC Publications, Geneva, 1994, p. 124, 126.

13. The Orthodox theologian Anastasios Yannoulatos, Archbishop of the Orthodox Church of Albania, has been engaged in missionary work in Albania trying to re-build the Orthodox Church. In addition to his missionary activities, especially in Africa, Yannoulatos has for a long time been an active member of the WCC. See his collection of essays, a welcome contribution to Orthodox Christian theology and to the wider ecumenical movement: *Guidelines on Dialogue with People of Living Faiths and Ideologies*, WCC Publications, Geneva, 1979; Idem, *Facing the World. Orthodox Christian Essay on Global Concerns*, WCC Publications/St. Vladimir's Seminary Press, Geneva Crestwood, N.Y., 2003; Idem, *Universality and Orthodoxy* (Παγκοσμιοποίηση και Ορθοδοξία, Akritas, Athens, 2000 (in Greek).

limited compared with that of men, consisting for the time being at least of isolated instances rather than constituting a policy on the part of the major world religions of promoting the emancipation of women and their active participation in making decisions and effecting interventions. Inter-religious dialogue as understood and promoted today in the world, especially in the three Abrahamic religions –Judaism, Christianity and Islam– is marked by a low participation of women. This becomes abundantly clear when one peruses the proceedings of inter-religious conferences and examines the persons involved and the relevant publications.

One finds that participation and publications by women are exceptions to the rule. Ursula King, Professor Emerita and Senior Research Fellow of the Institute of Advanced Studies, University of Bristol, England, referring to the role and presence of women in inter-religious conventions, wryly observes,

> The evidence of women's absence is further highlighted by the visual documentation of many interfaith meetings. One only has to look at the photographs of the meeting of religious leaders in Assisi, or at those of any other official gathering to be shocked into the realization that all ecumenical events, whether inter-denominational or inter-religious, are dominated almost exclusively by male representatives of the human race. Can these "religious leaders" today still legitimately "voice" the concerns of women and speak on their behalf, as if women could not speak for themselves?[14]

These conclusions were the rule until at least the late 1980s, when the WCC slowly but surely began to include increasing numbers of

---

14. Cf. her article *Gender and Interreligious Dialogue*, first presented in February 2004 at the Nanzan Institute of Religion and Culture in Nagoya, Japan. It is an updated, revised version of her earlier article "Feminism: the Missing Dimension in the Dialogue of Religions" in John D'Arcy May (ed.), *Pluralism and the Religions: The Theological and Political Dimensions*, Cassell, London, 1998, p. 40-55.

women in such meetings[15]. The first decisive steps in this direction were taken with the beginning of the Ecumenical Decade of Churches in Solidarity with Women programme (EDCSW, 1988-98). This was an opportunity for the churches to promote the activities of women in society and to extend solidarity to them. Thanks to this initiative, Christian women of various denominations began to meet, forming regional ecumenical organizations[16].

Our own meeting today here in Volos (Greece) is one of these initiatives, held as part of the programme Women in Church and Society of the WCC. The purpose of this meeting is to evaluate the participation of Orthodox women in the ecumenical movement past and present, and to plan and organize future initiatives and activities to strengthen the presence of Orthodox women in the ecumenical context. Thanks to this meeting of Orthodox women, we have had the opportunity to meet, to get to know one another, and to inform ourselves about the activities and the status of Orthodox women around the globe—under the umbrella of the WCC and with the kind support of the Academy of Theological Studies of the Holy Metropolis of Demetrias in Volos[17].

15. As early as 1982, The Ecumenical Forum of European Christian Women (EFECW), an international, church-related organization, active in 30 countries of Europe and in which women from every Christian denomination participate, was funded. See http:// www.efecw.net. In 2005, a non-profit organization was formed in Athens called "The Ecumenical Form of European Christian Women—Greek Branch" (Οικουμενικό Φόρουμ Ευρωπαίων Χριστιανών Γυναικών-Ελληνικό Τμήμα).

16. For further information on the Ecumenical Decade of the Churches in Solidarity with Women, see the WCC website: http://www.wcc-coe.org/wcc/assembly/decfest.html.

17. A conference in Volos (8-12 June 2008) entitled The Participation of Women in the Ecumenical Movement: Past, Present and Future, in collaboration with the Women in Church and Society programme of the WCC. The website of the Volos Academy for Theological Studies-Holy Metropolis of Demetrias: http://www. acadimia.gr Here one can see the reasoning behind the meeting and read the history of the beginnings and the course of the Orthodox Women's Consultation under the aegis of the WCC.

Unlike inter-Christian meetings, however, inter-religious networks of women enjoy little support and publicity. The WCC has come to appreciate the need to promote such networks, and it is fortunate that we are seeing an increase in the promotion of inter-religious meetings. It is our privilege to participate in one such meeting. This is a three-year joint workshop of Muslim and Christian women entitled "Women as Peacemakers through Religion", the first international network of inter-religious dialogue organized by Christian women representing various denominations and Iranian Shiite Muslim women.

The first such meeting took place in Tehran in November 2007, jointly organized by the WCC in Geneva and by the non-governmental Institute for Inter-religious Dialogue (IID) in Tehran. At this four-day scientific meeting, we conferred with Iranian women working in numerous disciplines and specializations, including directors, journalists, physicians, psychologists, university professors, theologians and sociologists, as well as young women students from various universities in Tehran. The Christian side was represented by Protestant women from various churches of Europe and USA and Orthodox women from the Church of Greece and the Syriac Orthodox Patriarchate of Antioch. The purpose of this network is to demonstrate women's potential for understanding and experiencing religion in their respective communities. The meeting contributes to the Decade to Overcome Violence 2001-2010, a WCC initiative that promotes peace and non-violent coexistence[18].

The second meeting was held in September 2008 in Sweden and hosted by the Diocese of Gothenburg. During this meeting, the members of the workshop met with members of the Church of Sweden and engaged in dialogue with local groups on such subjects as new ways and means for women to practice inter-religious dialogue. Iranian Muslim and Christian women had the opportunity to exchange life experiences with Swedish families, focusing on subjects

18. "Decade to Overcome Violence 2001-2010," International Ecumenical Peace Convocation website: http://overcomingviolence.org.

in which the participation of women may be critical in building the peace. The four-day meeting in Gothenburg contributed to further strengthening bonds and creating interpersonal relationships[19]. There were also some concrete results from the meeting in Gothenburg, as the group developed detailed plans for three projects to be carried out in 2009 in the areas of media, health and inter-religious education.

The *media project* focused on establishing a website that will serve as a tool of communication for the group and with other inter-religious and women groups. This website provides the names of all the women in the network, together with brief resumes, the talks presented both in Tehran and Gothenburg, and a number of interviews conducted during these meetings.

In the *health project*, members of the group from Iran have begun implementing an action plan concerning HIV/AIDS prevention. This group proposed six major activities: i) to prepare educational material on HIV/AIDS prevention in Iran; ii) to organize orientation meetings in Iran with religious people, decision makers and policy makers in order to create a support group for this project; iii) to organize a one-day workshop, "Training for Trainers". This final project will involve 30 technical persons, from governmental organizations and NGOs, each of whom will work with 30 trainees in multiple workshops. The trainers shall select 30 peer educators (for example, a prisoner giving workshops in prison). The workshop will be evaluated in September 2009, and will include suggestions and plans for future. This project will be posted on the network website.

The *educational project* will develop a guide that will include four case studies of women engaged in inter-religious dialogue in different contexts and their contribution to peacemaking in Bosnia, Iran, Sweden and the USA. The studies will be accompanied by papers reflecting on different aspects of the dialogue that took place within

19. "Women as Peacemakers: Christian-Muslim women workshop", Retrieved from http://www.oikoumene.org/en/news/upcomingevents/ev/se/browse/1/article/1722/ women-as-peacemakers-chr.html.

the group. Finally, this guide will incorporate a feminist analysis of dialogue methodologies practised by women at the grassroots level.

Another goal is to organize a larger inter-religious women's gathering with special focus on the role and contribution of women to peacemaking. Besides this workshop, other meetings of women in the Middle East have begun. Thus, in January 2009, during a Christian-Muslim meeting in Cairo, a similar group of women started planning the launch of an Arab Dialogue Group for Christian and Muslim Women, which hopefully will work closely with the above-mentioned network in the future. Similar regional initiatives have taken place and are continuing in Africa, South Asia, Europe and the USA, and it is hoped that by the end of 2009 the Christian-Muslim network will be ready to share its work, enlarge the network and plan for the future[20].

For our part, we believe that as women's inter-religious networks develop further, inter-religious dialogue will take on a truly ecumenical dimension, bringing action in line with theory. I cannot neglect the dynamic presence at these meetings of African women, whatever religion they belong to, who have the strength to face the enormous problems with which their countries struggle (social, financial, gender etc.), to raise their voices and demand a better future for their daughters.

20. This information was provided by the coordinator of the workshop, Miss Rima Barsoum, who is a programme executive for Christian-Muslim relations of the WCC. I would like to extend my special thanks to her for her tireless efforts to provide information, and for her commitment and belief in inter-religious dialogue. For her, inter-religious dialogue is more than a theological meeting; it is primarily a testament of people of different faiths who live and work together and who share responsibility for the good of humanity. Finally, her involvement in the delicate question of Islamo-Christian dialogue is valuable, for her Syrian background has taught her to co-exist with the religious other and to engage in dialogue in the spirit of reconciliation and love.

II. WOMEN AS SOURCES OF INSPIRATION

ELIZABETH BEHR-SIGEL: HER VISION AND CONTRIBUTION
OLGA LOSSKY

Introducing Elisabeth Behr-Sigel to a meeting of the World Council of Churches (WCC) is challenging for me, especially when I guess that most of you met her during the previous gatherings on the role of women in the Church, or at least have perhaps read one of her books. Let's recall together that Elisabeth was one of the pioneering thinkers on this subject. It all began when she gave an introductory lecture at the famous Agapia meeting in 1976. On that occasion, she made a first appeal to women: "I think that it should be good that Orthodox women emerge from their silence, which has been imposed on them not by the ecclesial Tradition but by customs and social conventions". From then on, she led a deep and systematic investigation on the place of woman in our Church, both practically and ideally. She thus quickly became known as the specialist on the question of the ordination of women, and, as we know, was invited all over the world to expound her opinion.

Today, however, I would like to share Elisabeth with you in another light. I emphasize that when she attended Agapia and began working on this new subject, she was 69 years old, meaning that she already had an important career of a theologian and thinker behind her. It was perhaps as a result of her rich life experience and mature outlook that she was able to tackle this new subject. Towards the end of her studies, in the 1930s, she had had the opportunity to be a Lutheran pastor in a little village parish in France for almost a year. Elisabeth is one of the first women pastors in history: she led the church service, she preached, and she visited her parishioners, with whom she developed a real friendship. Her reflection on the role of women in the Church starts from this very practical experience, and later from her own parish life in the Orthodox Church. However, she implanted her understanding of the subject within the context of a deep knowledge of the Holy Scriptures and the Fathers of the Church.

Elisabeth had a gift of drawing attention to burning issues: why should discrimination exist with regard to the roles of men and women in the Church, since we are all called to the same aim: deification? How can we say that a man holds a function by virtue of his nature or simply because it's always been like that? And lastly, how would we define the priesthood of women, and should it be an ordained one?

Elisabeth had her own personal way of considering such questions. This was due to her great capacity for analysis and expression, which was evident in her papers. I think that her theological analysis is characterized by two main movements: she wished to respect the Tradition and at the same time she expressed very audacious –and sometimes provocative– ideas.

But I would say that she was even more striking – not through what she said, but through who she was.

I had the privilege of meeting Elisabeth at the very end of her life, a year to the day before her death. A friend of mine had asked me if I was interested in interviewing her about her life. During the course of one year, I visited her about twice a month, on Saturdays. We took lunch together, which she insisted on preparing, and on these occasions she enjoyed telling me many anecdotes, which I recorded faithfully. For me, this was a very deep and enriching time, not only because I learned so much about the development of Orthodoxy in Western Europe during the time of her life, but because of the opportunity of getting to know her personally.

At 97, Elisabeth was amazingly full of life. An extraordinary faith in God was evident in her, and had been throughout the hard times she encountered: for example, during the second world war and through her husband's illness. She also had a striking curiosity for the contemporary world, which remained with her until the very last day of her life. Her primary concern was how the Gospel could be a living message for the people of today. She also had the gift of being able to care for each person she met in a unique manner, especially those who suffered unjustly. From this point of view, she was sensitive to the marginalization of women in her church and wanted to promote a better place for them, according to their abilities.

I must confess that before I met Elisabeth Behr-Sigel, I never felt that the place of women in the Church needed special attention. Now I realize that the privilege of such a situation is thanks to Elisabeth's patient fight. In the various parishes I often go to, the previous generations have made an effort to raise awareness about the necessity for everybody, regardless of their gender, to find their place and role in the community using the gifts God has given them. And I think this effort has really born fruit in many Orthodox parishes of Western Europe.

When Elisabeth passed away, I had hours and hours of recorded tapes of her voice. Her family gave me access to all her archives. Thanks to this and to the testimony of her friends and relatives, I was able to write a first story of Elisabeth's life, entitled *Vers le Jour sans déclin* (Towards the Day without End). It was published by Le Cerf in French in 2007, to mark the centenary of Elisabeth's birth. It will also soon be published in English by Notre-Dame University Press in the United States.

Throughout the writing of the book, I have tried to illuminate how all of Elisabeth's life converged towards an encounter with Christ, which was the focal point for her action and thought. To conclude, I would say that Elisabeth's main heritage concerning the question of woman in the Church could be summed up in these words: Let's be audacious in our reflection and in our action; let's be open-minded; we must go as far as possible; but at the same time we must keep in mind our Tradition. We must not be afraid to question Tradition, with the trust that we will find there the answers to current matters on the participation of women in the life of the Church.

INSPIRATION, DISAPPOINTMENT, AND A WAY FORWARD: MOTHER ERENE AND THE CONTRIBUTION OF ORTHODOX WOMEN TO THE ECUMENICAL MOVEMENT

PHOEBE FARAG MIKHAIL

Inspiration and disappointment simultaneously describe my impressions as I left the World Council of Church's (WCC) Orthodox women's consultation in Volos, Greece. "Inspiration" is the best word to describe the women I met from so many different churches and the historic effort made by some of these women to pave the way for the leadership of women in Orthodox churches. I owe a debt of thanks to many of them for my ability to write and publish this reflection now in an ecumenical publication. However, the internal focus of the gathering disappointed me. The title of the consultation, "The Participation of Orthodox Women in the Ecumenical Movement, Past, Present, and Future", gave the impression that we were going to spend time discussing how Orthodox women could contribute to the wider ecumenical movement. Instead, the focal point of most conversations was the status of Orthodox women within the Orthodox communions. While these are still worthy and timely conversations to have, the outcome of the meeting, from my perspective, lacked a clear way forward for Orthodox women's contribution to the wider ecumenical movement.

"No matter how many times I said it," I wrote in my journal during my time in Volos, "…we never actually talked about how Orthodox women can actually contribute, as Orthodox, to the ecumenical movement as a whole. Every time I made that statement, people said 'well-said' and then went back to talking about Orthodox women's concerns. I wanted to see more balance in the discussion. The definition of ecumenism that I heard over the week had mainly to do with theology and less to do with using our collective voice and collective strength for effective social advocacy and social justice. That bothered me because I always understood the missions and outreach programs as one of the arms of the ecumenical movement, just like faith and order is."

Providentially, while reflecting on this outcome, I was reading the newly translated hagiographies[1] of Mother Erene, a contemporary female leader in the Coptic Orthodox Church who died in 2006. I found in the story of a nun dedicated to her convent, her monastic community, and her cell clear examples of how Orthodox women can make a strong contribution to the wider ecumenical movement. Mother Erene fully claimed the space of female monasticism in the Coptic Orthodox Church and pushed boundaries of women's leadership in the Church. During what is now known as the "Coptic Renaissance", she changed the reputation of the convent from a place to go for women who cannot find husbands to a place where space is coveted and beautiful, and where highly educated women pray for the opportunity to be consecrated.

Mother Erene (1936-2006) became the head of the Monastery of St Mercurius (Abi Seifein) at the age of 26. Her saintly life, her strong relationship with the saints, and the miracles that surrounded her made her a popular and well-respected figure in the Coptic Church during her life and after her death. Her story reveals a depth of spirituality that came from her early relationship with the poor, and a visionary leadership style that focused on building a community of love among the sisters in her convent and beyond it. Social justice, community and effective leadership emerged as key to the success of her ministry, and, I believe, key to the role for Orthodox women in the ecumenical movement.

1. *Tamav Erene: The Jewel of Heaven and the Beacon of Monasticism*, The Convent of the Great Martyr of St. Philopater Mercurius "Abi Sefein" for Nuns, Old Cairo, Egypt, 2007; and *Tamav Erene and Glorious Horizons in Monastic Life Part I*, The Convent of the Great Martyr St. Philopater Mercurius "Abi Seifein" for Nuns, Old Cairo, Egypt, 2008.

SOCIAL JUSTICE

Two figures in her early life made profound impressions on Mother Erene: her grandfather and her mother. In addition to generously giving money to the poor families in their vicinity, Mother Erene's mother would also take them into account in her daily cooking, sending her daughters to secretly distribute food to the families before sitting down as a family to eat. When her daughters asked why she distributed food when money surely was enough, she replied, "They would buy the bare necessities with the money we give them, but they won't cook this kind of food"[2].

Mother Erene's grandfather, a wealthy business owner, showed similar daily devotion to the poor. She describes his influence on her in her own words,

> I remember my childhood very well; it is printed in my memory… I used to get in the cab with him; it was filled with different kinds of fruits and vegetables as well as envelopes full of money. He used to get off himself before every house, and I would do the same, to knock at the door. When he heard the sound of the door latch signifying that the door was about to be open, he would quickly put whatever he had in front of the house and disappear immediately without being seen by anyone[3].

These two models of devotion to the poor had two things in common: first, they treated the poor as equals to them, and second, they did their work in secret. Mother Erene's mother made food for the poor as if they were part of her own family. Her grandfather did not send any of his workers to distribute the food and money; he went himself to their doorsteps. These acts –while charitable in nature and certainly not examples of a sustainable, rights-based approach to development–

2. *Tamav Erene: The Jewel,* p. 39.
3. Ibid. p. 52.

did exemplify important social justice principles. Their toil in secrecy exemplified how working in social justice is not an afterthought or a place to seek personal glory, but an exertion of daily effort with the oppressed rather than above them.

Mother Erene quickly applied these principles when it came to creating an order for her monastery. When she first became consecrated as a nun in 1954 (at age 18), the Monastery of Abi Sefien had a part communal, part reclusive order. The nuns met once a day for prayer at sunset and otherwise remained in their own cells for prayer, responsible for their own clothes and their own meals. When she became the head of the monastery in 1962, she spent three days in fasting and prayer to receive direction. After a vision that directed her to read the Pachomian Koinonia and with the approval of the then-Patriarch Pope Kyrollos VI, she implemented the Pachomian communal order in the monastery – not without resistance from older nuns. This order included nuns meeting several times a day for prayer, working with their hands, wearing a common dress and eating at a common table. Mother Erene described one of the concerns she had about the original order of the monastery before she changed it,

> The vendors used to visit the Convent with their own merchandise, and each nun would leave her cell to buy what she needed… it upset me to see a poor nun unable to buy only a little when a rich one could buy as much as she wanted… In truth, I was upset by the striking differences between the nuns. The richer nun was comfortably off, while the poorer one was destitute. If a nun worked with her hands and received help from her family, she led an easy life, whereas if she could not work and had no outside help, she had to struggle in poverty[4].

The lessons she learned in her childhood rendered Mother Erene unable to bear seeing inequality exercised in the monastic community she was

---

4. *Tamav Erene and Glorious Horizons,* p. 32, 37.

leading, and the Pakhomian order enabled her to rectify this. In addition to abolishing the visits of vendors and creating a common table for meals, nuns were obliged to put all their financial gifts from their families into a common fund that supported the whole convent community.

COMMUNITY

The implementation of the Pakhomian Koinonia did not just create social equality among the nuns in the convent; it also created a community of nuns supporting and encouraging one another. "While it is up to each nun to decide on the level of austerity appropriate for her," Mother Erene has said, "our life is still essentially built on partnership and love."[5] Before the beginning of any communal prayer, the nuns in the Monastery of St Mercurius would confess to each other, "I have sinned, forgive me". This daily act of humility prevented division among the nuns in the community.

Early in the implementation of the new communal order, Pope Kyrollos VI anticipated that there would be great resistance to Mother Erene from the older nuns in the monastery. He had ten particular nuns in mind and he wrote a letter to Mother Erene telling her that if she experienced any troubles with these nuns, he would allow her to order that they leave the convent. Mother Erene, however, had made a promise to herself from the day she became the head of the convent: "I would put up with any nun with love until the very last day, regardless of the troubles that she might cause me"[6]. She informed the Patriarch that she would not need to ask any nun to leave the convent[7].

5. Mariz Tadros, "A life like no other", *Al-Ahram Weekly*, 8-16 April 1999, Cairo, Egypt.
6. *Tamav Erene and Glorious Horizon*, p. 39-40.
7. Interestingly, the Pachomian Koinonia allows for monks to be expelled from monasteries; St. Pachomious himself expelled monks (A. Veilleux, *Pachomian Koinonia, Volume 1, Cistercian Studies 45*, Cistercian Publications, Kalamazoo, Michigan, 1980, p. 150). However, the nuns at the Monastery of Abi Sefein have indicated that Mother Erene drafted a different document based on the Pachomian rule, and the rules of this document were applied to the monastery (Pieternella van Doorn-Harder, *Contemporary Coptic Nun*, University of South Carolina Press, Columbia, 1995, p. 58).

The elder nuns, in fact, inspired Mother Erene to have three altars built inside the convent so that the sisters could partake of the divine liturgy on a regular basis, rather than leaving the convent to do so at a nearby church. Some of the older nuns were unable to walk to the nearby churches and would wait for the priest to bring them communion. One particular nun, Mother Theodora, who was blind and unable to walk, wept for being unable to actually participate in the divine liturgy even though communion was brought to her. Cases such as Mother Theodora's created a sense of urgency for Mother Erene, and within one year of her leadership, the first altar was consecrated inside the convent – the altar of Abi Sifein. It was said that during the first divine liturgy celebrated in that altar, Mother Theodora was able to see and walk again.

By the grace of God and using the gifts he had given her, Mother Erene built a strong and cohesive community of nuns that continued to grow. It reached a point where there were no more cells to house the young women who were coming to the monastery to be consecrated nuns. To resolve this problem, Mother Erene built two sister convents in other parts of Egypt and acquired and built on the land adjacent to the convent in Old Cairo, known as the "old convent". She also organized the schedules of the nuns so that they could rotate between the three sister monasteries for times of refreshment and retreat.

LEADERSHIP

The community Mother Erene built in her convent extended far beyond the walls of the Monastery of St Abi Sefein. Three nuns in her community went on to become the mother superiors of other convents, thus showing how Mother Erene's leadership and discipleship empowered others to become leaders. One possible way she did so was by engaging them in the decisions made by the convent. While her hagiography does not describe many participatory processes, it does describe one way she engaged the nuns in the idea of expanding the monastery,

> When our beloved Mother first thought of establishing a new convent in the desert, she asked the nuns to ask fervently in

their personal prayers for the Almighty Lord to reveal His will. She also asked the community to dedicate both the Third Hour liturgical prayer[8] to the same subject. When we asked her why she chose this Hour in particular, she replied, "For two reasons. Because the Holy Spirit must guide us in every step we take, and because the Hour starts with the Psalm, 'May the Lord answer you in the day of trouble'"[9].

This was not a mother superior who made decisions without the knowledge of the rest of her community, but one who told them from the start her ideas and visions and asked them to pray with her. This type of leadership was described by one journalist and political science professor as democratic: "Mother Ireni doesn't run a convent like a traditional mother superior – she emphasises the importance of leading a community in a democratic way. 'I don't like to point to the sisters' faults and shortcomings. Words of love and encouragement are more effective'"[10].

Mother Erene capitalized on the talents of the nuns in her community by appointing some nuns to carry out research and writing work, conduct weekly Bible studies for their fellow sisters, and publish books out of the monastery. One significant and well-researched book published by the convent is *The Virgin Mary and Other Virgins in Different Ages* (Cairo: Harmony Printing House, 2002), a "feminist and new historical reading" about the role women played in the monastic movement since the early church[11]. Having read the book on my way home from Volos and learned the stories of many early church mothers I did not know about, I can attest to the importance of this work.

Mother Erene demonstrated participatory leadership outside the

---

8. This refers to the "Third Hour Prayer" in the *Agpeya,* the Coptic Church's *Prayer Book of the Hours.*
9. *Tamav Erene and Glorious Horizon,* p. 84.
10. Tadros A life like no other" *Al Ahram Weekly,* 8, 16 April 1999, Cairo, Egypt.
11. Heba Sharobeem , "A Modern Desert Mother", *Al Ahram Weekly* 16-22 November 2006, Cairo, Egypt.

monastery as well. Her popularity grew so great that she began to hold weekly public meetings during which she would recount stories of miracles, prayer, paradise and repentance that she had experienced, witnessed herself, or learned firsthand from others. She would often state in these meetings that she did not give sermons, but only told stories. I listened to a tape of one of these public meetings. She had asked all the participants to write down on a piece of paper what time would be most suitable for them to participate in the public meetings. "Then we will gather all the papers and choose the time most suitable for the majority," she said.

Participants also regularly brought pieces of paper with prayer requests to give to the nuns in the monastery. She explained to them exactly what was done with these pieces of paper: "Just so you are aware, we have a committee of four nuns that collect all the requests. They write down the requests on larger sheets of paper – the names of sick people on one paper, the names of people with problems on another, the names of people who have issues at work on another ..." In this way, she demonstrated unusual transparency about the monastery's activities.

Another tape also demonstrated how well-respected Mother Erene was by the priests and bishops of her time. On one occasion, she was invited to speak at St George's Church in Heliopolis, Cairo, soon after a tragic bus accident in 1999 that claimed the lives of 31 young people[12]. She had seen a vision of these youth and was told by her father of confession to share that vision with the surviving families. When she finished her talk, she asked His Grace Bishop Maximous of Medinet el Salam to comment on her words. His only response was, "I have no comment. I am here to learn".

Mother Erene humbly commanded the respect of many hierarchs in the Coptic Orthodox Church, who recognized her wisdom and depth of spirituality, including their graces Bishop Roess (a general

---

12. Jail an Halawi, "The carnage must end", *Al-Ahram Weekly*, 19 July-4 August 1999, Cairo, Egypt.

bishop), Bishop Misael of Birmingham, UK, and Metropolitan Ar-sanious of el Minya[13]. Although only priests and bishops are allowed to anoint people with oil, Mother Erene was given the right to do so by the late His Holiness Pope Kyrrollos VI, which she continued to exercise as "people flock[ed] to see her, ask for her prayers and re-quest that she anoint them"[14]. In this and in many other ways, Mother Erene pushed the boundaries of her role as a female ascetic in the Coptic Orthodox Church. She was regarded as a spiritual leader well beyond the walls of her monastery. She also literally expanded the walls of her monastery, building two sister monasteries as mentioned above, and empowering the nuns in her monastery to become leaders of other monasteries as well.

MOTHER ERENE AND THE ECUMENICAL MOVEMENT

How can Orthodox women forge a way forward in the ecumenical movement? Mother Erene gives us a vibrant example. Her life high-lights three important areas: social justice, community and leadership. Orthodox women already claim spaces in these areas, and they can push their boundaries, as Mother Erene has done. Orthodox women can work together and with other communions in the ecumenical movement for social justice. They should continue to build commu-nities, but must ensure that these communities bridge continents and Orthodox communions. Finally, they should not be afraid to demon-strate effective, empowering leadership in their home communions and within the ecumenical movement.

Social Justice. The majority of the world's poor are women and girls,

13. L.M. Bishoy Mikhail, personal communication, 14 December 2008: "My hus-band, Bishoy Lamie Mansi Mikhail, has a sister who is a nun at the Monastery of Abi Sefein. She has been there for the past ten years and has shared many experiences with Mother Erene with us".
14. Tadros Mariz "A life like no other" *Al Ahram Weekly*, 8, 16 April 1999, Cairo, Egypt.

with Amnesty International citing the figure at 70%[15]. Just as it "upset" Mother Erene to see inequality in her monastic community, so too should it upset us to continue to see poverty and inequality in our communities. Orthodox churches know poverty well. Their patriarchates are most often based in post-communist countries rebuilding themselves or other developing countries such as Ethiopia, India and Egypt. As Orthodox women, we cannot stand by and see so many of our sisters and brothers living in the world this way. And because of the unique role our mother countries play in our churches and in our lives, we have an intimate knowledge of poverty and working with the poor that we should build upon. One of our ecumenical contributions thus should be to increase advocacy with our sisters and brothers living in poverty around the world, and to share the intimate knowledge and experience with poverty that we have through our churches. In many Orthodox church contexts, working with the poor is one of the spaces in which women can take leadership roles, and in which Orthodox women have important experiences to share. I would like to see the next ecumenical gathering of Orthodox women spend significant time talking about how we can contribute to the social justice work of the ecumenical movement in a more proactive way.

Community. During the consultation, I also learned about several worthy online networks for Orthodox women, most of them based in North America. These communities are wonderful ways to share resources and become connected, and I believe that we should increase the scope and breadth of these communities to connect more Orthodox women around the world. At gatherings like those of Volos, we are always educated and enriched, mainly through the conversations we have and witness between women from different Orthodox communions. However, as more than one participant pointed out, a large portion of the participants at Volos came from North America.

15. Irene Khan, "Neither Violence against Women Nor Poverty Are Inevitable." Amnesty International, 25 November 2008. http://www.amnesty.org/en/news-and-updates/feature-stories/neither-violence-against-women-nor-poverty-are-inevitable-2008/11.

Increasing the diversity of these meetings would only enrich them and build a stronger sense of community among Orthodox women around the world.

In addition to strengthening and increasing communities among Orthodox women across communions and oceans, we should also be encouraging active Orthodox women to expand their reach and participate in their local Christian ecumenical bodies. The richness of our church and the experiences we have serving within it should not be hidden. We should encourage each other to document our work and share it with other Christian communions within the ecumenical movement. Currently, for example, I am working on gathering the curriculum and evaluation for what is becoming a yearly event conducted by the Coptic Orthodox Churches in the Northeast and Mid-Atlantic regions of the United States. "Just As I Am" is a one day retreat for girls and young women focused on increasing their self-esteem and empowering them to live Christ-centered lives by focusing on their being created in God's image. Once I have gathered all the materials, I will be sharing them with the Justice for Women Working Group of the National Council of Churches of Christ in the USA. Just as we stand to benefit from the many resources of other Christian churches, so they stand to benefit from the wealth of resources and living examples we have in our own communions. In this way we can truly start to build a Christian community based on "partnership and love", in the words of Mother Erene.

Leadership. Mother Erene is just one contemporary example of effective female leadership in the Orthodox churches. The fruit of this effectiveness was not just the mother superiors who came out of her monastery, but also the Christian witness she was able make throughout the world through her story and even through the various illnesses she underwent before she reposed. There are countless other examples like Mother Erene, and we should use our platforms of communication to continue to share these, and other inspiring stories with each other, as well as to practice such leadership lessons ourselves. We should continue to empower others within our communities to become leaders, and our leadership should win others to Christ. Prayer, love, participation and building community were all characteristics of Mother Erene's leadership style that we should adopt as our own.

We should also fully claim the spaces open for women in the Orthodox Church to take leadership roles. By doing so –and by doing so using Mother Erene's humble, attractive and effective leadership example– we can start to push the boundaries of those spaces as Mother Erene has done. Although these may seem like spaces traditionally afforded to women, if they are not claimed through our active participation, they might be eroded. Mother Erene's example shows that even in the most traditional and enclosed space, that of a female monastic, one woman's influence can make changes well beyond her physical sphere.

"Many women were also there..." (Matt. 27:55). This verse, the theme of the consultation, is an appropriate way to think about Orthodox women's participation in the ecumenical movement: past, present, and future. My contemplations about a way forward for Orthodox women could only be take place *because* many women were there, ministering to Christ during His ministry, witnessing to Him after his resurrection, and receiving the Holy Spirit with all its gifts to all the disciples and apostles, male and female. May we encourage many more women to be there, ministering to the body of Christ, witnessing to him throughout the world, and using the gifts of the Holy Spirit graciously given to us, through leadership, through solidarity with the least privileged, and through community with one another.

III. LOCAL VOICES AND INITIATIVES

WOMEN THEOLOGIANS IN EUROPE: A CHALLENGE
Katerina Karkala-Zorba

L iving today in the common house of the European Union, we are all invited to exist under the same roof. But what is the kind of Europe we want to live in? This is the theme we propose to treat with respect to the following questions,

- What is the place of Christians in Europe today?
- What is the contribution of women in Europe, and especially Christian women and women theologians? What could the contribution of Orthodox women be?
- What kind of Europe do we want to live in, and what is the place of foreigners, migrants and refugees in Europe?
- How can we realize a dialogue with other religions in Europe?

WHAT IS THE PLACE OF CHRISTIANS IN EUROPE TODAY?

We live in the second millennium after Jesus Christ. But we are not always aware of the words we use in our date system. There is a meaning behind the "after Jesus Christ". First of all it means that our era, our civilization, has as a departure date the nascence of Jesus Christ. Even if we do not agree with the formulation that the roots of Europe are Christian[1], we have to admit that Christians are the founders, or at least the constructors, of Europe, as we know this continent today.

But Europe is also an image in ancient Greek mythology. Europe (in Greek *Evropi*) was a lovely young girl with a large front and a large view (from the Greek words *evri* and *opsi*). She was so lovely that Zeus, the father of all gods, saw her and fell in love with her. He captured her and brought her on a steer from the island of Naxos to Crete, where he entered into a divine marriage with her. But many things

---

1. His Beatitude Christodoulos, Archbishop of Athens and Whole Greece, «The Presence of the Church on the Horizon of Europe», in *Values and Principles for the Building of Europe*, Holy Synod of the Church of Greece, Athens, 2005, p. 477-83.

have changed since that time; the young girl has become an adult. Europe is now an old continent, the one that has given names to the other continents, like America and Australia, even if they did have anterior civilizations.

But what is the place of Christians in Europe? Can we still think in a selective way, as Christians, Muslims, Jewish? Can we not put our differences apart in order to be more efficient in a world that threatens to disappear (we only have to think of the ecological catastrophes)?

I think that we may no longer have the "luxury" to separate ourselves and to think in selfish and selective ways. We are not on islands, separated from one another, Christians, Muslims and Jews. Perhaps the Orient has always had another way to live, the multicultural and global. The famous town of Jerusalem is perhaps an excellent example of this. But in Greece we also have our own experiences of living with other religions. Perhaps it is time to think this over again and learn from one another.

The Orthodox Church is sometimes considered as being apart from the wider ecumenical dialogue. Perhaps this is so, since the Orthodox church has always had an "exotic" flavour. It is true that many Christians from the Roman Catholic and the Protestant churches do not know where to place us exactly. But also we Orthodox classify the Roman Catholic church and theology (like the Protestant churches and theologies) as the churches and theologies of the West. Perhaps this is the biggest difference we still carry with us as Christians since the time of the schism between the church of the Orient and the Occident. It is our different *modus vivendi*, our life-styles, our perceptions of everyday things that separate us much more than the major religious dogmas.

The place of Christians in Europe could have more weight if we would consider two major elements: first, cooperation with other religious communities in Europe, and second, acceptance of our mistakes of the past as Europeans and as Christians. By moving in the direction of these two elements we can accept our "Christian roots in Europe" and then see how much the "plant" of our continent has grown up.

WHAT IS THE CONTRIBUTION OF EUROPEAN WOMEN IN EUROPE?

The contribution of women on our continent is certainly very important. As a former co-president of the Ecumenical Forum of European Christian Women (EFECW) I could certainly give many examples. We may not always identify Europe with the image of Evropi in mythology or with a Jeanne d' Arc; but we have to admit that women have played an important role in our European history, even if it was not always visible. Women also played an important role in the history of the Christian Church. Women surrounded Jesus: Mary and Martha, the Samaritan woman, the women at the Cross and the women who brought myrrh to the empty tomb, women like Phoibe and Priscilla, and so many others in the meetings and the coming together "as Church" of the first Christians. But also in the history of the nascent church in the Orient, like that in the Occident, women were always the carriers of tradition from one generation to the next. Certainly we owe much to our grandmothers and mothers who raised us in faith and love for God and neighbour[2].

But what could the contribution of women and Christian women in Europe be? I do not think that it could be different from the contribution of men. In fact, only a community (*koinonia*) of men and women in Church and Society can provide a solution for the problems that threaten Europe and the world[3]. But it has also been important as women to have a voice and to gain rights that are essential for the recognition of women as human beings with the same value as men. In the Greek language, we have a difference in etymology between the term *isotita*, which means "equality", and *isotimia*, which means "of the same value". I do think that having the same value is more important in gaining a true equality between men and women[4].

Christianity can give to men and women a perfect equality: that

---

2. Mary T. Malone, *Women & Christianity, Volumes I, II, III,* Columba Press, Dublin, 2000. See also Leonie B. Liveris, *Ancient Taboos and Gender Prejudice: Challenges for Orthodox Women and the Church,* Ashgate Publishing Company, Hampshire, 2005.
3. Cf. Constance F. Parvey (ed.), *The Community of Women and Men in the Church: The Sheffield Report,* WCC Publications, Geneva, 1982.
4. See also Katerina Karkala-Zorba, "Women and the Church: A Greek-Orthodox Perspective", *Concilium* 3 (2006), p. 36-45.

is, the equality in Jesus Christ, where we have neither Jew nor Greek, neither slave nor free, neither male nor female, for all are one in Christ Jesus (Gal. 3:28)[5]. This is a form of equality that does not question the value of each human being, but also does not diminish it. It is exactly this equality that we are looking for as Christian women in Europe.

In Livadia in Greece in 1994, a conference was held with the theme "The Orthodox Woman in the United Europe"[6] organized by the then-Metropolitan of Thebai and Livadia and now Archbishop of Athens and all of Greece, Hieronymus II. One may read in the report of the European conference that the Orthodox woman is called to give today witness in Europe as a Christian woman and to transmit the values of family and life in Jesus Christ, such as Christian values and traditions. But she also has to have the possibility of accessing European institutions and obtaining, together with other women in Europe, situations of responsibility in a Europe of (at that time 15 and now) 27 countries.

Christian women however do have different voices in Europe. In the same report of the conference in Livadia, one may read that women have a multitude of possibilities to become active in the Church: in liturgy, in the parish, in monastic life, in society[7]. In 1988, an Interorthodox Consultation took place in Rhodes on the subject of «The Place of the Woman in the Orthodox Church and the Question of the Ordination of Women»[8]. The conclusions of the report of the consultation state that the Orthodox Church wants first of all to preserve the dignity of the human person, created in the image and likeness of

---

5. Cf. Evanthia Adamtziloglou, *Neither male nor female...*, (in Greek) Simbo Publications, Thessaloniki, 1998.

6. Agathaggelos Charamantidis, Holy Metropolis of Thebe and Livadia, *The Orthodox Woman in United Europe* (in Greek), Report of the European Interorthodox Conference, Epektasis Publications, Katerini 2001.

7. Ibid., p. 338.

8. Gennadios Limouris (ed.), *Ecumenical Patriarchate of Constantinople: The Place of the Woman in the Orthodox Church and the Question of the Ordination of Women*, *Interorthodox Symposium, Rhodos, Greece, 30 October-7 November 1988*, Tertios Publications, Katerini, 1992.

God, in the face of the tragic dehumanization we often encounter in our contemporary society. «Any act which denies the dignity of the human person and any act which discriminates against women and men on the basis of gender is sin»[9]. However, in Rhodes, as well as in other meetings before Rhodes (Agapia/Romania in 1976[10]) and meetings after Rhodes (Damascus in 1996 and Istanbul in 1997), we have to discern the signs of the times and guarantee the full participation of women in the Church[11].

Certainly there are differences concerning the ordination of women[12]; the Protestant churches in Europe have ordained women as pastors and bishops since the last century (for example, in the United Kingdom, in Germany and in the Scandinavian countries). The Orthodox Church knows about the ordination of deaconesses, known in the Church from the first millennium, and there were efforts to reintroduce it in the last century[13]. In October 2004, the Holy Synod of

9. Ibid., p. 28.

10. Constance J. Tarasar, Irina Kirillova (eds.), *Orthodox Women, Their Role and Participation in the Orthodox Church, Report on the Consultation of Orthodox Women, September 11-17, 1976, Agapia Roumania*, WCC Publications, Geneva, 1977.

11. Kyriaki Karidoyanes-FitzGerald, *Orthodox Women Speak, Discerning the "Signs of the Times"*, WCC Publications/Geneva, Holy Cross Orthodox Press, Brookline, Massachusetts, 1999.

12. On Women's Ordination see Ian Jones, Janet Wootton, Kirsty Thorpe, *Women and Ordination in the Christian Churches: International Perspectives*, T & T Clark, 2008, where: Katerina Karkala-Zorba, "Ordination of Women from an Orthodox Perspective", p. 54-75.

13. See Evangelos Theodorou, "The Ministry of the Deaconess in the Greek Orthodox Church", in *The Deaconess*, WCC Studies, Geneva, 1966; Kyriaki Karidoyanes FitzGerald, *Women Deacons in the Orthodox Church, Called to Holiness and Ministry*, Holy Cross Orthodox Press, Brookline Massachusets, 1999. See also: Thomas Hopko (ed.), *Women and the Priesthood*, St. Vladimir's Seminary Press, New York, 1999; Anne Jensen & Grigorios Larentzakis (eds.), *Diakonat und Diakonie in frühchristlicher Tradition*, Grazer Theologische Studien Nr. 23, Graz 2003. On women and priesthood see Konstantinos Yokarinis, *The Priesthood of Women in the Ecumenical Movement* (in Greek), Tertios Publications, Katerini, 1995.

the Church of Greece decided to re-institute the order of deaconesses. It remains to be seen whether this will remain a fact only for women in monastic communities, or if it will be applied to female theologians and married women.

In 2002, the Church of Greece founded the Special Commission on Women's Issues. After two meetings in central Greece (October 2004) and in north Greece (February 2006), an inter-diocesan women's network is now ready to be applied. We also need to utilize the human capacity between women theologians, who have superior studies in theology (post-graduate degrees or PhDs). Those female theologians, like their male colleagues, are occupied in the field of education. Some will have the opportunity to work in research and teach at a university. Only a few will work at the level of the dioceses, where the clergy has priority.

However, we do find in the Orthodox Church, like in other Christian churches and religious communities, that women work on a voluntary basis in the parishes and in the socio-philanthropic areas of the church. Orthodox women do have their own visions and voices[14]. The question would be how much volunteer time of women we still can count on, given that today women do often have their own professions along with their family and personal lives. These are some of the questions the churches certainly have to ask themselves, and provide the answers to[15]. Certainly there is a place in the Orthodox Church for discussion of the question of feminist theology, as it exists in the faculties of theology in the West. In the Diocese of Demetrias, the academic courses at the Academy for Theological Studies during the winter of 2002-2003 offered the theme of "Gender and Religion: The Role of the Woman in the Church". There, we discussed the subject: "Is there a place in Orthodoxy for a feminist theology?"[16] We have to

14. Eleni Kasselouri & Sophie Deicha (eds.), *Women's Voices and Visions: Orthodox Women,* WCC Publications, Geneva, 2006.
15. Cf. Dimitra Koukoura, *The Place of the Woman in the Orthodox Church and Other Study Texts of Ecumenical Reflection* (in Greek), Publications Sfakianaki, Thessaloniki, 2005.
16. Katerina Karkala-Zorba, "Is there a place in Orthodoxy for a Feminist Theology?» (in Greek), in: *Fylo Gender and Religion, The Place of the Woman in the Church,*

dare to speak the truth on subjects that might help us to continue to preach the Gospel of God in a more and more secularized world[17].

In order to finish this item on the role of women in Church and Society, I would like to mention a great Orthodox woman theologian, who is no more among us: Elisabeth Behr-Sigel. Among her studies, books and articles on the role of women in and for which she was not always well received, I would like to refer to her book *The Ministry of Women in the Church,*

> This clarification is to be carried out within the dynamic and authentic Tradition and not in rupture with it. Tradition's dynamism comes from the Spirit sent by the Father and who rests on the Son. Like living water the Spirit flows from the Son onto women and men and makes them God's daughters and sons, and the creation waits in groaning and labour pains for their revelation (Rom. 8:,19-22).[18]

WHAT KIND OF EUROPE DO WE WANT TO LIVE IN?
WHAT IS THE PLACE OF FOREIGNERS, MIGRANTS AND REFUGEES IN EUROPE?
AND HOW CAN WE REALIZE A DIALOGUE WITH OTHER RELIGIONS IN EUROPE?

It is however uncertain that we all do want the same Europe. For one

Indiktos, Athens, 2004, p. 209-42. See also Eleni Kasselouri-Hatzivassiliadi, *Feminist Hermeneutics* (in Greek), P. Pournaras Publications, Thessaloniki, 2003.

17. See Ioannis Petrou, "The Question of Women in Church Tradition", *Anglican Theological Review* 84.3 (2002), p. 645-67.

18. Elisabeth Behr-Sigel, *Le ministère de la femme dans l'Église* (English translation), Les Éditions du Cerf, Paris 1987, p. 172-73; idem, *The Ministry of Women in the Church*, translated by Steven Bigham, Oakwood Publications, Redondo Beach California, 1991, p. 164-65; cf.: idem, *L'ordination de femmes dans l'Église orthodoxe*, Éditions du Cerf, Paris, 1998; Elisabeth Behr-Sigel & Kallistos Ware, *The Ordination of Women in the Orthodox Church*, Risk Book Series, WCC Publications, Geneva, 2000; *Orthodox Church in America, Women & Men in the Church: A Study of the Community of Women and Men in the Church*, Department of Religious Education, Orthodox Church in America, New York 1980; Deborah Belonick, *Feminism in Christianity: An Orthodox Christian Response*, Department of Religious Education, Orthodox Church in America, New York, 1983.

thing, it is community based on economics. The EU is all for facilitating the commerce and the relations between the member states. Certainly the decisive moment was the second world war, which led to so many catastrophes and devastations for our old continent. But from the creation of the European Community in 1949 to today, we have grown together as Europeans and we are convinced that Europe, in order to be a true continent and a community of countries which are distinct but united, has to go on a search for its own tradition and history. This was also recognized by Jacques Delors, who proclaimed the programme "Soul for Europe".

A meeting of the EFECW in July 2000 in Thessaloniki/Greece was on the theme of "Searching for the Female Soul of Europe: Myth or Reality?" The conference was greeted by all Christian churches, and it was emphasized that "we must stop downgrading the women's face, stop the trafficking in women and that we must absolutely protect the unemployed, the homeless, the socially excluded, the raped and the abused women"[19].

We do want a Europe where no one would be excluded because of race, gender, religion, origin, etc. – a Europe that respects human rights and that also reveals a social politic[20], that could embrace all people and provide them with the possibility and the right to employment and a life of dignity. This equality of rights and opportunities for men and women was a campaign of the European Union, launched in 1996 from the European Commission and the European Parliament[21].

But there is a long way to go from rights on paper to rights in reality. The religions in Europe certainly have a large role to play in the near future. We see every day in the news conflicts created because of religion. Often these conflicts are classified religious, even though there are other reasons: political, economic etc.

---

19. Message from His Beatitude The Archbishop of Athens and All Greece to the Conference of the EFECW in *Forum Newsflash*, Special Issue (Fall 2001), p. 4-5.
20. Cf. "The Lisbon Treaty of the EU", Europe: http://europa.eu/lisbon_treaty/full_text/index_en.htm.
21. Commission européenne, *Égalité des droits et des chances pour les femmes et les hommes dans l'Union européenne*, Office des publications officielles des Communautés européennes, Luxembourg, 2002.

However, it is important to underline the fact that religion is making a comeback in Europe, and that the churches have to be prepared to receive the "other", the different, the one who speaks another language. We have to respect them as human beings with full rights to life, dignity and liberty. The foreigner, the migrant, is the neighbour Jesus asked us to love as ourselves. And for the application of the divine commandments, we all are needed: clergy and laity, men and women, old and young. Let us take this opportunity –given to us in another time– and put it into action in Europe today.

THE ST. NINA QUARTERLY:
BRINGING TOGETHER A COMMUNITY
OF ORTHODOX CHRISTIAN WOMEN
TEVA REGULE

I would like to begin with the words of Elisabeth Behr-Sigel, of blessed memory, describing the reality of the Church today. Her words describe the thoughts of many in the Church, especially women. Over the years, they have continued to resonate with me more deeply,

> Here is juxtaposed and joined the liberating message of the Gospel and archaic taboos, a theological anthropology both spiritual and personal, [and, I might add, one which I find very life-giving] and the misogynistic stereotypes inherited from patriarchal societies[1].

As we all know, the Orthodox church traces its origins to Christ and the apostles, and it takes this inheritance seriously. But how do we discern the Truth of God embedded within the various cultural manifestations of the Church from the human limitations of that culture in place and time? How can the community uphold Tradition and be what Jaroslav Pelikan, a well-respected Church historian, describes as the "living faith of the dead" without slipping into "traditionalism", which he describes as the "dead faith of the living"[2]. How can the Church become the "Church", a vehicle for all to enter into the life of Christ? It was in trying to address these questions honestly and prayerfully, especially with regard to the ministry of women in the Church today, that the St. Nina Quarterly was conceived – striving to be an example (as my dogmatics professor suggests) of the Church as a "therapeutic, healing community".

---

1. Elisabeth Behr-Sigel, "Women in the Orthodox Church," *The St. Nina Quarterly* 2 (1998), p. 1.
2. Jaroslav Pelican, *The Emergence of the Catholic Tradition (100-600)*, University of Chicago Press, Chicago, 1971, p. 9.

We started as a small group of Orthodox women from a variety of ethnic backgrounds who, through friendship and a growing women's network, found one another. Some had known each other for years and others were meeting for the first time. Many of us had studied at seminary and had earned advanced degrees in theology. However, few were working in the Church in a capacity for which they were trained. Also, we soon discovered that, because the Orthodox Church in North America is grouped primarily along ethnic lines, our contact and communication with one another was limited at best. Therefore, the journal would not only need to explore the ministry of women in the Church, but would also need to include the experiences of all Orthodox women, regardless of ethnic group or jurisdiction. We sought the assistance of several well-respected Orthodox theologians, including Bishop Kallistos Ware and Elisabeth Behr-Sigel and others of various dioceses and jurisdictions. They eventually became our honorary advisory board. So, with a sense of mission, hope, and admittedly, little money, the *St. Nina Quarterly* was born.

As our mission statement says, the *St. Nina Quarterly* is a publication dedicated to exploring the ministry of women in the Orthodox Church and to cultivating a deeper understanding of ministry in the lives of all Orthodox Christian women and men. Our mission is the discovery and cultivation of these gifts for the nurturing of the entire Body of Christ. To this end, we will strive to educate, inform and provide space for an ongoing, creative dialogue aimed at reaching across all boundaries to support and encourage the growth and vitality of the God-given ministries of all of our sisters and brothers in Christ[3].

We began in 1997, building each issue around a theme and focused on ideas and subjects specifically of interest to Orthodox women as well as to the Church at large. Some of the themes of past issues have been "Women in the Church – Past, Present, and Future"; "Wo-

---

3. For more information about the *St. Nina Quarterly*, see my article in the *Ecumenical Review* 53.1 (January 2001).

men in the Early Church"; "Women in the Church as a Reflection of Society"; "Mary as an Icon for all Humanity"; "Women and the Creation Stories"; "Language and Imagery in the Church"; "A Tribute to Our Foremothers"; "Our Faith and Body and Mind"; "Our Faith and Our Praxis"; and "Our Faith and Community". In each issue we attempted to increase our awareness of our roles as persons made in the image and likeness of God within the entire community of believers.

In the journal, we have carefully examined our theology and Scripture, especially the creation stories and the writings of St Paul. We have also examined the history of women's participation in the life of the Church, including the early Church roles of prophetesses, the orders of virgins and widows, and ordained female deacons. We looked at women's participation in the Church in various cultural traditions, including the ancient Byzantine and Syriac traditions, as well as more modern manifestations. We highlighted the lives of saints and other noble women as models for us to emulate – both in the early Church, including Macrina the Younger, sister of Basil the Great and Gregory of Nyssa (4rth century); Nina, Evangelizer to the people of Georgia (3rd century); and Catherine of Alexandria, Christian apologist schooled in the classics (2nd century); and those of more recent times, including *Gerontissa* [Elder] Gabriela, a Greek woman missionary to India and Africa; Mother Maria Skobtsova, a Russian-French woman, and defender of the poor and the persecuted (especially the Jews in France during the second world war); and Mother Alexandra, the former princess of Romania and founder of one of the first women's monasteries in the United States. Moreover, we collected a number of stories and interviews of the senior women among us in honor of their lives, accomplishments, and service to the Church. Their stories represent a written record of an oral history that might otherwise have been lost.

In addition to examining the past, we also focused on our lives in the Church in the present, examining liturgical practices regarding women and the sanctuary (including the ritual churching of infants and mothers and participation of girls as altar servers) and the female diaconate[4]. We also tried to spotlight and uplift the ministry that women are already doing in the Church – as chaplains, missionaries, and educators and, in its liturgical life, as readers, chanters, choir directors, homilists, hymnographers, and iconographers. We tried to inform our readership of conferences and retreats concerning women, including the proceedings of various conferences sponsored by the World Council of Churches (WCC) for Orthodox Christian women – Agapia, Romania (1976), Damascus, Syria (1996), and Istanbul, Turkey (1997) and other international gatherings in Sophia, Bulgaria (1987), Rhodes, Greece (1988), and Crete (1990), as well as local conferences and retreats. We published interviews with respected Orthodox theologians and reflected on various issues of our day, including spiritual life, monasticism, language in the Church, feminism, anthropology, peace and justice, and Christian dialogue and unity.

Due in part to the expense of publishing a printed journal and mailing it around the world, we decided to focus more on developing our presence on the internet. In 2005 we launched a website that contained all the back issues of the printed journal, as well as a fledgling online journal of presentations, articles, sermons, interviews, reflections, poems, book reviews and event summaries. We have spent the past year upgrading the site and hope to unveil it later this year. We plan to include a forum for online discussion, a question and answer box, a speakers' bureau to publicize the qualifications and areas of interest of Orthodox women retreat leaders and conference speakers, as well as many new articles and postings.

Although discussion lists are not yet available on our website, we have used e-mail to inform and encourage Orthodox women and men

---

4. The churching of the child is founded on the practice of offering the first born (male) child to God based on Mosaic Law (Ex. 13:2, 12, 15). For instance, Jesus was presented to God in the temple in Luke 2:22ff. Although in the early church, all baptized infants were taken into the altar area at this time, today only the male child is routinely taken into the altar area while the female child is taken only so far as the entrance. We are happy to say that this policy is slowly changing to treat male and female infants equally.

to respond to pastoral issues that arise in the Church. By doing so, we have found solidarity with one another.

Indeed, many of our readers –women and men– have begun to find a sense of community with one another through the *Quarterly*. Although our readership is based in North America, we have readers in countries throughout the world. Women living in the traditionally Orthodox countries of the former Soviet bloc can now study their faith more freely and read about their Orthodox Christian sisters in the West. By learning about women in our history and by looking at our theology, especially as it relates to our practice, we hope that those who have felt isolated from the community of believers can reconnect, that those who are physically distanced have found kindred spirits with whom they can correspond, and that all of us, learning from one another, have found a community of interrelationship and shared love.

In the fall of 2000, the *St. Nina Quarterly* (with support from the Council of Eastern Orthodox Churches of Central Massachusetts) sponsored our first conference entitled, "Gifts of the Spirit". This was the first time that Orthodox Christian women (and some men) gathered in the New England region to explore the ministry of women in the Church. The gathering offered an opportunity to meet other Orthodox Christian women, exchange experiences and ideas of ministry within the Church, grow in understanding of ministry, and further explore the various ministries of women in the Church.

It was a tremendous success! Although originally envisioned as a regional event, the conference attracted women from all over the United States. They came from many different ethnic jurisdictions and parishes, and ranged in age from teenagers to women in their 80s (we had quite a few mother-daughter pairs). Some had graduate degrees in theology, some were faithful women in their parishes who had never studied theology formally. We were a diverse group, but we all gathered as one in Christ. We formed new friendships and renewed old ones. We shared experiences and feelings. We discussed and debated theology. We lived, shared and exalted in the gifts and ministries of women in the Church. It was an exhilarating experience for many of the participants.

In May 2003, we sponsored our second conference entitled, "Discerning the Signs of the Times" with the French Orthodox theologian and "grand dame" of Orthodox feminism, Elisabeth Behr-Sigel. It was an opportunity to meet someone many have called, a true "mother of the Church". We had the opportunity to hear of her formative ecumenical experiences during the second world war in France, where she first encountered the Orthodox Church, as well as her experiences as a keynote speaker at the first international consultation for Orthodox women at Agapia Monastery, Romania, in 1976, and as a participant at subsequent conferences sponsored by the WCC. We also had the opportunity to discuss the future of the "role of women" in the Church, including the re-establishment and rejuvenation of the ordained female diaconate, an office that is in the history and tradition of the Orthodox Church.

In September 2004, members of our editorial board assisted our parent organization, the Women's Orthodox Ministries and Education Network, and board member Demetra Jaquet in a conference focusing on lay ministry in the Church. This included highlighting the many ways in which women are already serving the Church. We also explored the history of the female diaconate and what it might look like in the 21st century (We have also assisted our parent organization in conferences in July 2006 in England and October 2006 in Minneapolis).

At each conference we strive to be "Church" – a community of interrelationship and shared love. We gather at the Liturgy as the "Body of Christ", worshipping God and experiencing a taste of His future reign while still in history. We gather as community to read Scripture, live the Tradition of those who have gone before us, and receive the Eucharist of the risen Christ. We use our gifts to minister to one another –building up that Body– as the "Temple of the Holy Spirit". And we provide the space to be the "therapeutic, healing community" that is the Church. It is only in such a community that we can experience the love of God in this world as fully as in the next.

I conclude by paraphrasing the thoughts of one participant at the celebration of the Divine Liturgy at our "Gifts of the Spirit" conference,

> [It was] the most beautiful, peaceful, prayerful, uplifting Liturgy that I had ever attended. I felt connected to Christ as never before, praying in a community with so many women using their gifts for the glory of God – iconographers, hymnographers, chanters, readers, homilists...

Our model of Church is the Holy Trinity. It is a beautiful and life-giving understanding of our goal as a human community. It is our hope that our experience and our understanding of Church continue to grow towards this goal so that we can participate in the life that is union with God.

ST. CATHERINE'S VISION
Barbara Harris

St. Catherine's Vision (SCV) is the work of women theologians and many others striving to fulfill the mission of the Church. They are committed to three initiatives: Orthodox unity, spiritual renewal and religious education. Founded in a discipline of love, seeking the discernment of the Holy Spirit, St. Catherine's Vision strives to explore, study and work toward the "edifying of the Body of Christ" through Orthodox theology and ministry. SCV is a nonprofit organization. The board members represent the Orthodox Church in America, the Greek Orthodox Archdiocese, the Serbian Church in America, the Antiochian Archdiocese, and the Romanian Diocese. Its membership encompasses all jurisdictions in North America, including our Oriental Orthodox sisters and brothers. St. Catherine's Vision is the only such organization endorsed by the Standing Conference of Canonical Orthodox Bishops in the Americas (SCOBA).

SCV is presently engaged in efforts to bring together women graduates of Orthodox Theological Schools at the master's level and above, and has sponsored two retreats blessed by SCOBA to that end. The main focus of both of these efforts was to bring women together in a spirit of love to prayerfully discuss and discern their place in the world and in the Church as well as to encourage each other. Approximately two hundred women have graduated from Orthodox Theological Schools in North American since the 1960s. St. Vladimir's Orthodox Theological Seminary (SVS) and Holy Cross Greek Orthodox School of Theology (HC) are the primary seminaries that have admitted and graduated women. SVS has regularly admitted and graduated women (averaging no less than 2 to 3 per year) since the 1960s while HC has consistently admitted and graduated women (averaging 2 to 4 each year) since the 1970s. Bringing these women together in retreat had never been done in the forty years women have been graduating from theological schools.

The first retreat, in November of 2005, was held over three days at

Antiochian Village Retreat Center in Ligonier, Pennsylvania. Its beautifully wooded location offered an ideal respite from day-to-day life. The retreat format consisted of morning and evening prayer services, small group and large group sessions. The theme for the weekend was Ephesians,

> ...to equip the saints for the work of ministry, for building up the body of Christ, until we all attain to the unity of the faith and of the knowledge of the Son of God, to mature manhood, to the measure of the stature of the fullness of Christ, so that we may no longer be children, tossed to and fro by the waves and carried about by every wind of doctrine, by human cunning, by craftiness in deceitful schemes. Rather, speaking the truth in love, we are to grow up in every way into him who is the head, into Christ, from whom the whole body, joined and held together by every joint with which it is equipped, when each part is working properly, makes the body grow so that it builds itself up in love (Eph. 4:12-16).

The main objective of the retreat was to bring women graduates together in prayer and dialogue. Each day began and ended with prayer services.

Victoria Trbuhovich offered the keynote address, speaking of spiritual warfare through the example of a royal family in Serbia who confronted a Muslim invasion. Valerie Zahirsky delivered the SCV lecture (Verse 13). Iulia Corduneanu Curtright offered the Sunday homily. For such a historic gathering, safety and trust were high priorities and the participants concurred that this work was all accomplished in a safe atmosphere with honest and mutual respect. Of the 27 women who attended the retreat, all agreed that it was a well-organized and thoughtful gathering with a healthy combination of worship, talks, group sessions and fun. They expressed regret only that there was not enough time to get to know one other more deeply. These women expressed a desire to meet again in one or two years.

The most prevalent expectation that women came to the retreat with was the strong desire to see old friends and make new ones. They were hungry for interaction between and among theologically educated women: to see how others are using their degrees and to ask how they can use their knowledge and experiences for the future.

The second retreat for women graduates was held in August of 2007 on Cape Cod at the Sacred Hearts Retreat Center. The setting was serene and welcoming, with wooded walking trails and a beach offering another way to be close to God in the colors, sights and sounds of his creation. Discussion at this retreat focused on articles from *Encountering Women of Faith: Volume I*, the first book published by SCV. The stories of the lives of some of the saints included in the book sparked lively conversation about the Church today and the ways that women continue to serve. Like other dedicated Orthodox women, those who attended the retreat are eager to use their gifts in the many ways that our rich Tradition has invited them to do for centuries.

The goal of this retreat was to build upon the relationships from the first retreat and to welcome new participants. As a direct response to the first retreat, more "down" time was worked into the schedule to allow women to get to know each other. Participants worshipped together each day in the chapel and met for Bible study in the library.

The first article discussed was "St. Olympias, the Deacon". A lively talk ensued regarding the Orthodox understanding of ordination. Clarification was provided about the non-portability of ordination as it is born from a need in a local community. Also discussed was the official blessing of ministries in which women are currently engaged.

The second article was "St. Xenia the Fool for Christ" and the talk that followed focused on identifying and responding to abusive relationships in all their forms (family, friends, work and church). This was an especially intense discussion for those who had experienced various forms of abuse, and it raised the level of awareness of all of the participants. There was discussion on the importance of including this particular topic in seminary education (how to identify and address these situations in a responsible manner as well as where to turn for help). Again, the twenty participants expressed a desire to meet again within a year or two and to meet for a longer period of time.

While bringing together women graduates is important, it is only

the first phase of SCV's efforts toward Orthodox unity, spiritual renewal and religious education. The intent is to expand the sphere
of outreach as time and resources allow. SCV is neither an exclusive
club of women graduates nor an Orthodox women's movement. This
would be self-serving and in direct opposition to Orthodox ecclesiology.

Individual members of the board were surprised to have discovered something about themselves through SCV meetings and retreats: that is, the passion shared for service as theologically educated
women. This has been life-giving work that has helped the members
individually and collectively to find their voices. Another important
effect of these efforts has been that participants feel more connected
individually and collectively in their ministries.

An SCV consultant and renowned Orthodox author described her
encounter through two perspectives: one was an intimate encounter
with her personal faith as she meets these holy women; and the other
is a broader view, as she sees anew the ways women have served in
the Orthodox church in the past and today. She said that the authors
helped her engage with the saints by bringing new dimensions to the
essays. Each author was asked to "research responsibly... discern a
particular spiritual prism, discipline or Christian practice to which
the life of their subject of study gave witness... and reflect personally
how this unique witness touched their own lives...", and this reader
found the results to be rich and edifying.

While conducting retreats, SCV has concurrently engaged in efforts of religious education – authoring one book, as mentioned above;
with volume two in production; and with a third book in development (which will be devoted to engagement with the Theotokos). The
second volume of Encountering Women of Faith, like the first, will
be a collection of chapters written by SCV members reflecting on the
lives of women saints. Through the prism of Orthodox hagiography
(specifically women saints) the writers relate these saints' stories to
the lives of modern women and to their own personal faith and their
relationships with God and with other people. In this way, they will
engage the reader in a deeper understanding and practice of the Or-

thodox faith. A special feature of the book is a series of discussion questions at the end of each chapter. Saints Mary of Egypt, Thecla, Perpetua, Felicitas, and Maria Skobtsova are among those who will be discussed.

The SCV website (http://www.orthodoxwomen.org) contains updated information about board members and current initiatives.

JOURNEY TO THE PROMISED LAND
MARIA KHOURY

It is so difficult to write sometimes, because I really don't know where to start. Do I start at the beginning, even before my creation, with the thought that I was with God and there was some type of special plan for me so I ended up in the Holy Land? Or do I begin with where I was born, in Tripoli, Greece.

I am proud of my Greek ethnicity, but I was taken by my parents from the village to the United States for better educational and job opportunities – only to marry a husband there who would bring back to the village. However, it is not an ordinary village that I am in right now, as I sit on the highest mountain region of Palestine on the West Bank of the Jordan River overlooking the Dead Sea. At night I can see the lights of Jerusalem shining, and on the other side, the lights of Amman, Jordan. I am truly in the one and only 100% Palestinian Christian village left in this region, after Christianity survived over two thousand years of wars and bloodshed in the sacred land in which our Lord was born, lived, was crucified and was resurrected, and where Christians make up less than 1.6% of the total population.

When I begin to feel sorry for myself as a Greek-American in the middle of the wilderness and among people who are nothing like me, where Muslims and Jews slaughter each other over the plight of the Promised Land, I simply look down at the Jordan Valley where Mary of Egypt spent more than forty years of her life. I try to muster up some courage and strength from her devotion to the Lord, made to clean her soul and seek forgiveness.

She came to this Promised Land just for the fun of it, for a free ride with pilgrims, who actually led her to a life-changing experience she never dreamed about imagined could happen – until she could not enter the Church of the Holy Sepulchre. It is documented in the Greek Orthodox Patriarchate that Mary of Egypt had a vision of the Virgin Mary, who instructed her to go beyond the Jordan River and seek forgiveness for her sins. Thus the story of this great saint has been used as a role model, especially during the Holy Lenten Season, for many centuries. But for me, geographically situated right above the Jordan Valley, the story of Mary of Egypt is a powerful reminder of the dedication and love people have for God.

The only comfort that I have in this small village, and the only connection that I can feel as an Orthodox Christian in the middle of nowhere, is that Christ walked into this area, known as Biblical Ephraim, right before His crucifixion. "Jesus therefore walked no more openly among the Jews; but went thence unto a country near the wilderness, into a city called Ephraim... " (John 11:54).

The village of Taybeh had the biblical name "Ephraim" in Judea. This was changed to its modern name by the Islamic leader Salahdin in approximately 1187. As the folktale goes, Salahdin visited the village Ephraim and found its people very hospitable and generous; thus, he stated that they were "Taybehn" ("good and kind" in Arabic) people. Since that day, biblical Ephraim took the modern name "Taybeh".

Our village of Taybeh is the only all-Christian village that remains in Palestine. It lies twenty minutes outside of Jerusalem, before the ancient town of Jericho, with less than 2000 residents, all of whom are Christian and the majority Greek Orthodox. All the residents are Palestinians, with a handful of outsiders.

Following the 1967 Israeli invasion of the West Bank, thousands of people from Taybeh emigrated to Australia, America and Europe because of the politics, the economic situation and the daily suffering faced under military occupation. The village is located between Jerusalem and Jericho, in the biblical land of Judea.

In the early 1990s, my husband, David, and his brother Nadim were greatly influenced by their family to return from Boston, where we were students at Hellenic College. He was urged to invest in Palestine, especially with the opportunities offered by the historic Oslo Agreement, where we hoped Israelis and Palestinians could co-exist and have a prosperous future together. After investing millions of dollars in the Palestinian economy and producing the one-and-only Palestinian beer, Taybeh Beer –which is actually the only micro-brewed beer in the entire Middle East area– we found ourselves living in a collapsed economy following the Second Palestinian uprising of September 2000, as the Israelis re-occupied the Palestinian territories.

Many families that had returned to invest in Palestine could not handle the checkpoints and daily shootings, and they returned to their host countries. But my husband and I continued to watch the Palestinian people seek freedom and self-determination, while he produced beer and I published children's books to help promote values and traditions of the Holy Orthodox Church. The newest of these books (also known as the Christina Books) is entitled *Christina Goes to the Holy Land*, and it promotes a Christian presence in Palestine. The first of the Christina Books (of which there is a total of seven) was *Christina Goes to Church*, which helps children understand symbolism. *Coloring with Christina* is also an effort to reach the pre-schoolers through the enjoyment of coloring the holy sites.

I found myself, a Greek-American mother, unable take my three children to school because of the hundreds of military checkpoints set up all around us to protect the illegal Israeli settlers who have been living on confiscated Taybeh land since the invasion of the West Bank in 1967. I found myself driving on roads created for Jews in order to by-pass the Arab villages, where at night Palestinians would kill settlers and in the daytime settlers would shoot Palestinians. I could be a target for either, since I was neither Palestinian nor Israeli. I spent several months physically shaking, like a drug addict, as I drove to school and back again. For several years I would leave my home at 6:45 a.m. never knowing if I would return in the afternoon. There is no other way to feel when people all around you kill each other daily and you could simply die by being in the wrong place at the wrong time.

Although I have always believed in Christ, since I was born into a Greek Orthodox family and raised by devout parents, this war situation in particular made me feel that my life on earth is meaningless and that seeking a life with Christ is what God calls us to do. I thought, "My life on earth can end at any moment, and besides the fancy house, the expensive jewelry, the luxury car, what treasures do I really have that are everlasting?"

The violence in our area was so intense and the checkpoints so many that I also lost my job as an educator with the Latin Patriarchate Schools and contributed to the 60% unemployment rate in Palestine. As an unemployed professional person, I fell into a deep depression, and felt even more depressed since my husband could not leave or did not want to leave this place and return to Boston. I grew up thinking that "family" is mom, dad and the kids, but in Palestine family includes the grandparents and all the aunts and uncles. My husband could not escape to freedom and leave his family behind. I really had to struggle to be an obedient wife, waking up every morning to a man I began to think of as my enemy but to whom, in front of God, I had made vows to honour and respect. I was frustrated that the extended family was more important to him than me. I am sure now this is the reason that Palestine has been emptied out of its Christian people since the creation of Israel in 1948 – when one person leaves the country, they take everyone else with them, the whole extended family or clan.

I find it so very sad when I frequently venerate Christ's Holy Tomb the most precious and sacred spot for Christianity, where Christ's Holy Resurrection took place and the miracle of the Holy Fire continues to take place every year on Holy Saturday. The Israeli tour guide will say to pilgrims, "I cannot go in there with you but I will wait right here". The holy places have become like museums, empty shrines, when we are in deep need to keep our Christian community here and have people worshipping the Lord in churches throughout the Holy Land. I don't object to an ecumenical presence in Jerusalem and sharing the land with everyone, but I promote specifically that Palestinian Christian people should have their basic human right to stay where they and their parents were born, and not be squeezed out by Zionist policies of creating a 100% Jewish homeland for Jews only.

I have tried to find some type of meaning in my life, living in a war, unemployed, and as a foreigner in a country I never really wanted to come to. I can list at least fifty reasons why I do not want to live in a Palestinian village. But the one reason to stay overshadows all the others, and that is my faith in God. I make every effort to trust in the Lord's plan for me and to understand why certain things have happened to me, which has allowed me take my next breath in moments when I felt like dying.

I try very hard to believe that when God shuts doors of opportunity for you, it means you have to open not just your eyes but your heart and soul to find the windows of opportunity in His Divine Plan for each and every one of us. These days, I truly feel it is only to give glory to God and to worship our creator. As humans, we are put here on earth to struggle, and through the pain and suffering to make efforts to speak to God. I truly believe I would be speaking to God less if I continued to live in my middle class house in Boston, taught at Boston University, took my children to hockey, soccer and Greek School and tried to have a beautiful vacation each summer. I would be so busy, tied to such a perfect and wonderful routine, that I would not need God. You do not need God when you are engulfed in the materialism of this world.

I know God through pain, suffering and struggling on all levels: physical, emotional, mental and spiritual. I know God because I tried to understand the road in life He put before me and how I could use my skills and knowledge to give Glory to His Holy name. I know God because I tried to carry my cross with faith and dignity, and when my cross was so heavy, God sent people who might have even been angels. They prayed for me, they inspired me with their personal faith in the Lord, they encouraged me to trust in God. They reminded me that God loves me and would never put me in a situation that I could not handle, because He truly knows my heart and strength. I know God only by pure faith. I know God only through others who have inspired me by their presence.

I know God because I have seen the light and have experienced the miracle of the Holy Fire. The ceremony of the Holy Fire is one of the most magnificent celebrations in the Holy Land, which has been overshadowed because of the violence and turmoil in this region. Living the cycle of death every day has made it even more important for Christians to celebrate Christ in our midst and place all of our hope in the Saviour. Through the many years of killing, people here have surely been living in the darkness of all evil. It therefore seems more important than ever to see Christ as the true light and to be inspired towards peaceful ways of co-existing. As it is written in the gospel of John, "And the light shineth in darkness; and the darkness comprehended it not" (John 1:5).

As a small Christian community in the Holy Land, we have a duty to share this message with the entire international community. To give hope to people who might be suffering from darkness in other corners of the world. At the Orthodox Easter service we sing, "You arose, O Christ, and yet the tomb remained sealed, as at Your birth the Virgin's womb remained unharmed; and You have opened for us the gates of paradise". During the ceremony, Orthodox Christians remember that Christ is the One Who has smashed the gates of Hades and opened the gates of Paradise, and gone before us! Seeing the life-giving Tomb of Christ is another reminder of our final destiny. As a small Christian community, we want to witness and reflect Christ's eternal love. We pray for peace and hope Jerusalem can be an open city of all faiths, so that Christian pilgrims from all over the world can come and be inspired and spiritually uplifted by the true light of Christ and share the richness of the Christian roots that exist in the Holy Land.

Marrying a Palestinian Orthodox Christian husband has taken me on a journey of a lifetime. However, on this long walk I realized that the Promised Land that I am living in now is not a physical entity and that the Israel that we sing and chant in our gospels is not the Israel on the ground – the guns, tanks and armored jeeps. As Christian people, we are the new Israel because we have been baptized unto Christ and received our Lord and Saviour. Our Promised Land is God's heavenly kingdom where we seek to be in the ever presence of Christ, the King of Peace. It is through our very presence here in the Holy Land that as Christian people we can promote nonviolent resolutions to oppression and condemn violence. It is very important to keep a Christian presence in the Holy Land, to witness for Christ's peace and love for neighbor.

Our current situation reminds us that Christians are called not merely to love God with all their heart, mind, soul and strength and their neighbor as themselves. These are the chief commandments of

JOURNEY TO THE PROMISED LAND

the Old Testament. But we Christians are called to hear the Lord of the New Testament and to fulfill His commands found in Matthew 5:44 "Love your enemies; Do good to those who hate you; Bless those who curse you; Pray for those who abuse you; Turn the other check to those who strike you".

The most frequently asked question is why I stay in the Holy Land with such violence when I have the financial and professional means to return any time to the United States. I think my gut reaction to this question is that I am doing my best to understand God's will in my life and follow it, because I often think that if I was following my own will, I would be drinking my kafedaki and taking nature walks in Tripoli where I was born. My fondest memory of Tripoli is as a six-year-old child during the resurrection service at Prophet Elias church, when my late father handed me a candle and said "Christos Anesti". Thus if Christ is truly risen, we must also rise with him in a new life with God, seeking to save our soul and to follow one of the most important commandments, "Love your neighbor as yourself".

And so I live day-to-day, trying to understand the gospel and, especially since 2000, making every effort to serve the church of St George in Taybeh as a volunteer, specifically for a housing project to help young couples build their first home. Thirty families were on the list to save about $100 each month (if they could) to be part of a housing cooperative that would help them obtain land to use from the Greek Orthodox Patriarchate in Jerusalem. A committee would fundraise to help assist these needy families, none of whom had the $50,000 necessary to buy their home. Nine years later, and finally –with the help of the Metropolis of Boston, the Virginia Farah Foundation as the largest donor, and many churches and individuals across the world– the first $90,000 was raised to start building these homes. Half of the members of the housing project, frustrated by the lack of funds since 1997, dropped out and withdrew their personal savings since the church did not have enough money to start the project. The twelve families that continued the hope were ideally supposed to contribute $12,000 each from their savings to match funds raised, and a few are still short and cannot come up with this amount.

The ground-breaking day for the housing project was the day I had prayed for many years. People across the world had prayed with me, and this is the reason I have been able to maintain inner peace and continue to serve the church in spite of the years of daily bloodshed and violence all around us.

On August 1, 2005, the land allocated by the late Patriarch Diodoros was leveled for six duplex buildings that would help house twelve families. In order to maximize job creation, six different contractors built the units, and all workers who specialized in this labor had temporary work from August 2005 to April 2006, when the outer structure of twelve homes was finally completed. The families are responsible for finishing their homes from the inside, because although we have tried every humanitarian organization, none seem to exist to help with building private homes. Given the number of years it took just to raise what my Catholic colleagues can raise in a week, I would probably need another lifetime to finish these homes, especially as we are in a deficit of $48,000.

However, I do believe in miracles and in great friends like Marilyn Rouvelas, author of *A Guide to Greek Traditions and Customs in America,* who helped me understand I must do a lot of ground work to help raise awareness about the Christian presence in the Holy Land. She trusted I could do this through books, inspiring the publication of *Christina Goes to the Holy Land* for children. This book walks the footsteps of Jesus with the message that Christians need help to stay in the Holy Land (www.saintgeorgetaybeh.org).

MIDDLE EASTERN WOMEN AND ECUMENICAL WORK –
AN ORTHODOX INVOLVEMENT
Maha Milki Wehbe

The title of our conference, the Participation of Orthodox Women in the Ecumenical Movement: Past, Present and Future, could not have been more fitting to the subject of my contribution, since I am an Orthodox woman in charge of an ecumenical women's desk. Before assuming my current position at the Middle East Council of Churches (henceforth MECC), I was appointed by my Patriarch to represent my Antiochian Orthodox Church in the Regional Committee of Women at the MECC and in the Advisory Group on Women at the women's desk of the World Council of Churches (WCC). Thirteen years ago, I was also delegated by my church to be the coordinator of the MECC women's programme in Lebanon.

In this way, my Orthodox involvement was moving in parallel with my ecumenical. This involvement was translated on the ground by the first large convention on women from the different Antiochian dioceses, which focused on their role in the church and the prospects thereof. Following this came two international Orthodox women's conventions in Damascus and Istanbul, sponsored by the WCC women's desk. What followed from all this was the opening up of a network of Orthodox women worldwide who were to operate in close cooperation with the WCC. Our present meeting is but a continuation of this great path. All of this was concurrently taking place with my being a coordinator of the clergy wives group at the Orthodox Archdiocese of Beirut. My ecumenical work was working hand-in-hand with my work with the women of my church, and I felt that my involvement in one was enhancing and consolidating my involvement in the other.

The scope of my ecumenical work has been on the local, regional and international levels. On the local Lebanese level, as the co-ordinator of the MECC women's programme, my work has been undertaken in conjunction with a committee formed of eight ladies from the different churches. The programme, which was instituted in 1977, aims at playing a two-fold role. On the one hand, it works to promote and consolidate the role of women in the church; and on the other, it aims to help them to develop a solid role in the Church and in society at large, and pushes them to play that role. As such, the programme works through awakening the potentials of women in the Church to promote a spirit of renewal and vigor in their respective churches, not in isolation from men but in conjunction with the different constituents of the Church. The importance of this effort was that the bulk of the work was taking place at the grassroots level, where hundreds of women from the different churches assemble in each area to discuss common concerns, open up to each other, and tackle important issues. Dozens of conventions, activities and workshops took place; the main theme permeating those spiritual gatherings in the past few years was "Women as Peace Makers". Simultaneously, leadership training workshops were being held for smaller groups. A major focus of many of them was violence against women, an issue that still has an impact on many women and children in the region. Moreover, spiritual retreats and prayer meetings were held to promote mutual awareness of women regarding the heritages of the different churches they come from.

On the regional level, where our churches are patterned along patriarchal lines, the work and strategy adopted on the local level is carried on and at the same time intersects with a similar orientation taking place in Lebanon, Syria, Jordan, Palestine and Egypt. Of course, each country has its specific characteristics. The purpose of the regional gatherings was two-fold: to forge solidarity and networking among women, and to shed light on many injustices and wrongs women suffer socially, on the judicial level, and in the church.

It is important to note that the status of women in my region has markedly improved on most levels: social, economic and even political. Women there are more aware of their rights and are fighting for them with a good deal of success. Christian and Muslim women sit together and tackle the injustices and issues inflicted upon them, both in the past and in the present. Some of the topics were discussed have been "Women and Citizenship", "Citizenship and Belonging",

"Women and the Culture of Peace", "Capacity Development of Women", "Women and Economic and Social Pressures", and the "Role of Women in the Ecumenical Movement".

On the international level, and since I was a member in the Advisory Group on Women at the WCC for two terms, I was working simultaneously as the liaison between the Middle East region and the WCC women's desk in Geneva, representing my Orthodox church. In conjunction, I served on the steering committee of the women's festival preceding the WCC general assembly in Harare in 1998, where I was in charge of an icon exhibition for women saints, as well as a facilitator for the many Middle Eastern women who participated in the festival. This came at the end of the Ecumenical Decade of Churches in Solidarity with Women (EDCSW), which witnessed team visits to our area, of which I was the organizer. Within the scope of the EDCSW, many activities took place in the region. In addition, I participated as a delegate from the Antiochian Patriarchate to the WCC general assembly in Porto Alegre, Brazil, in 2006. Among the many other international conferences I had the chance to attend, I was invited to participate in the Methodist and the Presbyterian general assemblies in the USA and in the quadrennial meeting for the World Day of Prayer in Toronto, Canada, in 2007, representing the WCC women's desk.

This tour de force cannot sum up all that is happening in the different countries and churches of my region or the extent of my involvement in the different functions I have briefly alluded to. The issue I have been always stressing in all of them is the importance of awareness and praxis. It may suffice to say that the opening up of women towards each other and vis-à-vis their rights and potentials was a visible sign of the impact of all this work. This has been due to the fact that the women who participate in these activities are women who are active in their respective churches. These women engage in our activities to enrich and be enriched by each other's experiences and outlooks. This grassroots mode of ecumenism is bearing fruit, and it promises to be more fruitful for the betterment of women and for the betterment of the churches and society at large.

"DIGGING" TOGETHER:
A GIFT OF THE ECUMENICAL MOVEMENT
VALERIE ZAHIRSKY

How does the rest of the world view us, the Orthodox, and our faith? Having participated in several international ecumenical meetings, I think about this question often. Having lived all my life in the pluralistic society that is the United States, I have an "American" perspective on the question.

One way the world sees us is through the words we use to describe Orthodoxy. For example, we say the Church is a hierarchy. There are those who see this as a negative word expressing a negative concept; it means that one person or group has authority over another, and can wield power over another.

But the Orthodox model for hierarchy is not any human situation. It is, rather, the Holy Trinity. Perfect in equality, perfect in love, perfect in union, the three divine Persons are nevertheless a hierarchy. The Son is begotten of the Father, and the Holy Spirit proceeds from the Father. This means that the Father is the source of both. The divine truth of hierarchy is imperfectly replicated in our human relationships, but it is our model.

If we could share this meaning of "hierarchy" with others, we would be helping them toward an authentic understanding of the Orthodox faith. And it can only be good for every believer to discover a richer and positive meaning for a word they may have distrusted or thought of as negative.

But it takes time to "dig into" faith words and create clear definitions of them, and it helps if you can do the digging with others who also want to find the best ways of defining and explaining them. The ecumenical movement, specifically the World Council of Churches (WCC), has provided the time and the chance to gather with those others to continue digging. At the meetings in Crete, Damascus and Istanbul that I attended, committed groups of women were given the opportunity to meditate and discern together, striving and struggling to find the best ways to express the Orthodox faith.

Another word used frequently in the Orthodox church, and which others sometimes are troubled by, is "obedience". Perhaps Americans are especially hesitant about this word, as was brought home to me by the story of a young woman who would like to become a deacon in her Protestant church. She is concerned about the fact that she might have to submit to and obey a clerical authority. Having met some nuns of Mother Teresa's order, she is critical not of their piety but of what she calls their blind submission, their obedience, to an imperfect human authority.

But once again, it's good to "dig into" the meaning of this word. Orthodoxy teaches that the obedience of priest to bishop, of monastic to superior, is for the obedient one's salvation. Once again, our model is not some human system designed to give one person power over another. Rather, our model is the Lord himself. Christ was "obedient unto death". He chose to offer obedience to his Father when he said, "Not my will but Thy will be done".

In terms of mortal human beings, Mary the Theotokos is often seen as the model of obedience. But hers, like the Lord's, was chosen, as we know from the annunciation. Mary did not simply give her assent the moment Gabriel spoke to her. She sensibly questioned what he was telling her, and then agreed to her exalted role in God's plan.

It's important to remember, too, that this woman is not the only one who was called to choose obedience. Joseph had to accept what he was told by the angel about the birth of Mary's child. The nativity icon, with its depiction of the devil tempting Joseph not to believe the angel, shows the difficulty of Joseph's choice.

The lives of some other Orthodox saints, far from reflecting blind obedience, give us examples of deliberate disobedience. St Maria Skobtsova of Paris and St Gorazd of Prague broke the law and defied the Nazis. Mother Maria did it by giving shelter to Jewish people and by distributing false baptismal certificates. St Gorazd attempted to take the full responsibility for the actions of Czech partisans, who had assassinated a Nazi official and took refuge in his cathedral in Prague. In honoring these saints, the Church acknowledges the ambiguity of obedience and gives it a definition far broader than "blind submission".

I hope that in the future the WCC will continue to provide opportunities to Orthodox women from all over the world to gather. I hope that those women, in turn, will use some of their time together to determine good ways of defining the words by which the Orthodox faith is expressed, and will share their definitions with other Christians. Knowing the way Orthodoxy uses these words may help others see the words in a new, more sympathetic way. That can be one way of strengthening the fellowship of faith, in which we all hope to share.

BIOGRAPHIES

SPIRIDOULA ATHANASOPOULOU-KYPRIOU holds a PhD in Systematic Theology from the University of Manchester, where she also lectured on Christian Anthropology and on Religion, Culture and Gender. She currently teaches "Studies on Orthodox Theology" in the Master's Program at the Hellenic Open University and religious education in secondary education. Her publications include various articles on theology and literature (for example, 'Beyond the death of the Christian novel: Literature as Theology', *Philotheos* 6 (2006) 48-60; 'Samuel Beckett's use of the Bible and the responsibility of the reader' in Gaye Ortiz and Clara Joseph (eds) *Literature and Theology: Rethinking Reader Responsibility*, New York: Palgrave Macmillan Press, 2006, 63-72), on philosophy of religion (for example, *Modern thought about religion*, Athens: Elias J. Barjoulianos Press, 2006), on religious education, and on the problem of religions in the public sphere, and finally on feminist theology.

ANASTASIA GKITSI is a PhD candidate at the School of Theology of Aristotle University of Thessaloniki. She holds a MTh from Chambesy, Switzerland. She has been working in secondary education since 2005 as a teacher of theology, history and psychology. She is a member of the academic team of the Volos Academy for Theological Studies and has published poems, and theological and literary articles in journals, reviews and anthologies. She has been involved in several ecumenical events, symposiums and training seminars concerning the ecumenical movement, inter-religious dialogue and the strengthening of youth participation in the ecumenical movement.

TAMARA GRDZELIDZE is a program executive within the Faith and Order Secretariat of the WCC in Geneva, Switzerland. She holds a DPhil from the University of Oxford and a doctorate in Medieval Georgian Literature from the Tbilisi State University and a doctorate honoris causa from the Faculty of Theology of the University of Bern, Switzerland. Among her publications are: *Georgian Monks on Mount Athos:*

Two Eleventh Century Lives of the Hegoumenoi of Iviron (Bennet & Bloom, London, 2009); *Witness through Troubled Times: A History of the Georgian Orthodox Church, 1811 to the Present"* (Bennett & Bloom, London, 2006) and *One, Holy, Catholic and Apostolic: Ecumenical Reflections on the Church* (WCC Publications, Geneva, 2005).

BARBARA HARRIS works, volunteers and pursues advanced studies in Theological Education and Non-profit Management in St. Louis. She is a graduate of Holy Cross Greek Orthodox School of Theology, has earned a Master's Degree in Non-Profit Management at Washington University and holds a Bachelor's Degree in Music Education with lifetime teacher certification in both Missouri and Illinois as well as provisional certification in elementary education.

KYRIAKI KARIDOYANNES-FITZGERALD is presently serving as Adjunct Professor of Theology at Holy Cross Greek Orthodox School of Theology. She is also a licensed psychologist and health service provider (MA) and is certified as a pastoral counselor (American Association of Pastoral Counselors) where she maintains a private practice in Sandwich, Massachusetts on Cape Cod. She has published many books and articles, which includes the book *Orthodox Women Speak. Discerning the "Signs of the Times"* (WCC Publications/Holy Cross Orthodox Press 1999).

KATERINA KARKALA-ZORBA conducted university studies in French and German at Thessaloniki and Orthodox Theology at the Institute of Saint Serge in Paris. She earned a Master's Degree in French as a Foreign Language in Paris in 1988 and a Master's Degree in Ecumenical Theology in Thessaloniki in 2003. She is a PhD Candidate in the Theological Faculty of the University of Thessaloniki and Orthodox Institute of the Ludwig Maximilian University of Munich.

ELENI KASSELOURI-HATZIVASSILIADI is a New Testament scholar. She teaches in the Master's Program *Studies on Orthodox Theology* at the Hellenic Open University. Since December 2007, she has worked in

Volos Academy for Theological Studies of the Holy Metropolis of Demetrias. She was a visiting lecturer at the Institute of Orthodox Theology in Balamand in the 2009-10 academic year, offering a seminar for N.T. Master's students on the topic "Women in NT". She was vice-president of the European Society of Women in Theological Research (1999-2001) and a member of the steering group of the WCC programme on Women's Voices and Visions on Being Church (2002-2006). She was also a member of the editorial board of the electronic bulletin *lectio difficilior* (www.lectio.unibe.ch) from 2002 to 2006.

MARIA (KOUREMENOU) KHOURY is the author of eight Orthodox children's books, including *Christina Goes to the Holy Land*. She is a graduate of Hellenic College (1982), Harvard University (1985) and Boston University (1992) with a PhD in Education. Born in Tripoli, Greece, she was raised in Denver, Colorado. She has worked closely with church leaders in Jerusalem as a WCC consultant (2004), and is the author of *Witness in the Holy Land* (http://www.holycross.com/ www.HolyCrossBookstore.com), a reflection on her personal experiences living under military occupation. Her articles have been published worldwide and translated to various languages.

DIMITRA KOUKOURA is Professor of Homiletics in the Department of Theology of the Aristotle University of Thessaloniki. She has written several books and studies, including *The Role of Woman in the Orthodox Church and Other Studies on Ecumenical Issues*, focusing especially on women's issues. For the past twenty-five years, she has been active in inter-Christian dialogue in the framework of WCC, and since 2003 she has represented the Ecumenical Patriarchate in the Faith and Order Commission, in the Standing and Plenary Commission, as well as in the Commission of Churches in Dialogue and the Conference of European Churches.

LEONIE LIVERIS is Adjunct Senior Research Fellow at Curtin University of Technology, Western Australia. She is trustee and board member of the Metropolitan Cemeteries Board and consultant and historian for the renewal and heritage of six cemeteries. Visiting Scholar at the WCC in 2001, she is a past president of the Council of Churches in Western Australia and served as executive officer for women's desk for the Australian Council of Churches Commission on the Status of Women from 1986 to 1992. Leonie was the editor of the international Orthodox women's journal *MaryMartha* from 1991 to 1998.

OLGA LOSSKY has pursued studies in Literature in Paris IV-Sorbonne and Theology in St-Serge-Paris (correspondence courses). In 2004, Olga published the novel *Requiem pour un clou* (Gallimard Publications), and in 2007, she prepared and published the biography of Elisabeth Behr-Sigel, *Vers le Jour sans déclin* (Le Cerf Publications).

FULATA MBANO MOYO is a Systematic Theologian; Church Historian; and gender and HIV and AIDS activist-academic. She is the current WCC programme executive for Women in Church and Society with a mandate to co-ordinate women's global work in all WCC's member churches in all the eight regions (North America, Latin America, the Caribbean, Europe, Asia, the Pacific, Middle East, Africa).

PHOEBE FARAG MIKHAIL is an active member of the Coptic Orthodox Church in North America, serving as the representative of the Coptic Orthodox Church to the Justice for Women Working Group of the National Council of Churches. On a full-time basis she is currently the Training and Evaluation Co-ordinator at Amnesty International USA. She represents Amnesty International USA and the National Council of Churches Justice for Women Working Group in the Women, Faith, and Development Alliance.

MAHA MILKI WEHBE is the co-ordinator of the Women's Program at the Middle East Council of Churches and head of the Public Gardens Department at the Municipality of Beirut, Lebanon. She is also a member of the National Committee of the World Day of Prayer, as well as member of the Fellowship of the Least Coin National Committee and co-ordinator of the Orthodox Clergy Wives Group at the Archdiocese of Beirut. Moreover, Maha is former member of the Advisory Group on Women at the WCC. She is married to an Orthodox priest and the mother of a 25-year-old daughter.

AIKATERINI PEKRIDOU is a PhD candidate at the Irish School of Ecumenics, Trinity College Dublin. She is member of the Volos Academy for Theological Studies, currently representing the World Student Christian Federation – Europe Region (WSCF-E) on the Churches in Dialogue Commission (CiD) of the CEC.

TEVA REGULE has served as managing editor of the *St. Nina Quarterly*, a publication dedicated to exploring the ministry of women in the Orthodox Church. Teva has been an Orthodox consultant to the WCC at both the Harare and Porto-Allegre assemblies and participated in meetings focusing of the Women Being Church initiative in Stony Point, NY and Geneva, Switzerland. A life-long student of theology, she completed the Master of Divinity degree at Holy Cross Greek Orthodox School of Theology in May 2007. She is presently in the Master of Theology program, focusing on liturgical theology.

NATALLIA VASILEVICH graduated from Belarusian State University, Law Faculty, Department of Political Sciences. She holds a Master's Degree in Political Science. She is a member of the editorial board of the journal *Palitycznaja sfera*. From 2002 to 2006 she was leader of one of youth Orthodox Fellowships of Belarusian Orthodox church in Minsk, and since 2004 she has been the editor of the Belarusian Christian website, "Carkwa" (http://churchby.info). From 2007 to 2009 she served as a regional representative of Syndesmos in Central Europe. Since 2009 she has been the Director of the cultural and educational centre, "Ecumena" and senior lecturer at the Belarusian Law Institute. Vasilevich has been involved in the ecumenical movement through World Student Christian Federation (European Region) since 2002 and has participated in several events organized by CEC and WCC.

VALERIE ZAHIRSKY is a graduate of St. Vladimir's Orthodox Seminary in New York (Master of Divinity) and of the Claremont Graduate School in California (Masters Degree in English). She writes Orthodox religious education materials for World Vision International, which distributes those materials to Orthodox churches in Eastern Europe and the Middle East. Valerie also travels to those areas to train teachers. She is a co-chair of the Department of Christian Education of the Orthodox church in America, and writes curriculum and trains teachers for parishes in the USA and Canada.

AGGELIKI ZIAKA is a History of Religions lecturer at the Aristotle University of Thessaloniki, School of Theology and holds a Doctorate from the Marc Bloch University of Strasbourg. She specializes in Islam and the Arabic and Islamic civilization, which she researched extensively at Strasbourg University; the Pontifical Institute of Arabic and Islamic Studies (PISAI, Rome); and the University of Amman (Jordan). Her research interests are Muslim theology and history, as well as the social, religious and political dimensions of Islam in the Middle East.

THE PRESENT PUBLICATION
BY WCC AND THE VOLOS
ACADEMY FOR THEOLOGI
CAL STUDIES *MANY WOMEN
WERE ALSO THERE...* WAS
TYPESET AND PAGINATED
AT INDIKTOS PRESS PRINTED
AND BOUND IN PRESSIOUS
ARVANITIDES A.B.E.E. IN
JULY 2011 FOR INDIKTOS
PUBLISHING HOUSE

Edition Number: **352**
Number of Copies
of the 1st Edition: **1.000**